GOOD GOD

A SURPRISING DIALOGUE
BETWEEN GOD AND A MERE MORTAL

BETTY GREEN

GOOD GOD

Edited & typeset by VISION unlimited

Published & printed by:
The Leiston Press
Unit 1, Master Lord Industrial Estate
Leiston
Suffolk
IP16 4XS

ISBN: 0-9538308-6-1

Dedicated to my dear old friend
John Kemp D.O.
through whose guidance I was led,
over forty years ago, to a simple path
of truth.

CONTENTS

CONTENTS

CONTENTS
— 2002 —

CONTENTS

Dear Reader,

Condemn me not for daring to suggest that I am in touch with God. I am no different from you; I have no special powers, I am not more intelligent than you. I do have an unshakeable belief, a real knowing that I am God's child.

You are no different. You are God's child also and deep down you know it. You can do what I do, namely, get in touch with God, for God is another name for Good, the Great Universal Intelligence.

When I learned not to be in awe of God he was able to speak to me and through me. God, Good, doesn't want us to look up to Him, It, but just to be part of Him, Her, It. It is our right, our privilege, our gift, to be able to be in touch with our maker, our parent, our higher self.

You can do what I do. Maybe you have to do a good deal of thinking and reading and preparation, but it need not take the forty odd years that it has taken me to find this Truth for yourself. It is a wonderful feeling; you feel as though there is no longer any need to struggle through this life on this planet. You left your original home to come here for a time, but though you cannot remember the details of that perfect home, you did not return here alone. There is always another soul looking after you, guiding you, but never interfering with your free will.

It is your free will now to put this book down, to say what you like about it, to condemn me or to love me. In so doing you will be condemning or loving yourself.

You can do what I do. If you remember, Jesus said, "the things that I do you can do also and better than I." That was a sweeping statement and we have not yet learned to do what he did – only rarely in the way of miracles in healing the sick. But we can be in touch with God like Jesus was because he knew God was all Good, his higher self, with whom he could get in touch at all times.

Read some of the books recommended at the end of this book, listen to some of the teachers and speakers who are mentioned. They can make us feel very humble, though there is evidently no need for us to feel humble; thankful, yes, very thankful for everything that comes into our lives for we are at all times remembering and learning.

Some of the meekest people we meet can teach us wonderful lessons. They so often seem to have very little of this life's necessities, let alone riches, yet they are calm, loving and wise. There is a Peace about them.

To do what I am doing I think you first need to have a great desire, then it becomes a compulsion, to get in touch with God, Good.

When you realise how badly wrong this world is going at present you feel an urge to do something about it. Some people are able to go abroad to do good work, some are so rich they can give of their wealth, but some of us can put our compulsion into words, knowing that they will reach many others in this form.

Those who know me well would tell you I am not eccentric, not a religious maniac, not pious. I am fun-loving, energetic, sincere and honest. I do not like injustice to myself nor to others, nor could I live in an unpeaceful atmosphere.

I have my worries; I try not to, but it seems human nature to worry. I adore my family and I am anxious when things appear to be going wrong for them.

I have learned that the best way of helping them is to pray for them – to speak to God about them. He already knows all that is happening, but it is a great comfort to talk to God. Then I listen and He tells me that He already knows all. I feel better for sharing my cares with this loving friend, all Good. He can sort things out in the Right Way, I might put a spanner in the works.

Dear Ones, do try this method of helping your loved ones, and not only your loved ones, but the whole world.

Television brings so much to our notice that we were quite unaware of in the past. I have been watching some heart-rending programmes about the very sick in parts of Africa. There are no drugs available because they cost too much, yet those drugs are sometimes used in the Western world just for cosmetic reasons. How awful. Those poor dears, many of them children, are suffering in terrible pain because there is no available help for them. It makes me ashamed to be alive. Have you seen these programmes? How does it make you feel?

What are we going to do about it? Can we continue just sitting back and hoping somebody else will go to their rescue?

Please pray for them. You do not know how? Then pray to God, Good, like this:

> *"Dear perfect God, Good, I hold all these suffering people in your Divine Light, a brilliant Light, so bright I cannot look right into it, but I know it is there. I concentrate on holding this Light over those souls and I picture help reaching them. I make a reality of it. I see others going to their rescue.*
>
> *I hold the enormous chemical companies all over the world in the Light, that they may have compassion, for there must be people working there who can pick up these thoughts. May many people hold these good thoughts.*
>
> *I make a reality of so many people going to the help of these suffering souls. I know you, God, can use these right thoughts and that they can annul and overcome the selfishness in the Western world, make us more aware of all the suffering we are causing. May we be ever thankful for all our blessings, for all that we have in our lives that we are apt to take so much for granted. We know that these prayers are heard for we are talking to you, Good, God."*

I know that God does not wish me to keep this new-found gift to myself. I share it willingly, lovingly and with humility to you all – for we are all One.

MY OWN EXPLANATIONS AND THOUGHTS

We have so much to unlearn. We have been brought up to fear God, to believe we shall be judged by God, to wonder if there really is Hell. I am astounded how many people I talk to doubt if there is anywhere after this life.

First read with your heart and mind, not with your brain, doubting. Know you are about to read the Truth and you will be able to confirm what I am privileged to tell you by reading some wonderful books, the names of some I will tell you later.

There is NO DEATH – not as we mostly talk about it and think about it. We should find new words for DEAD and DEATH because we conjure up a false picture and connect them with an end instead of a continuation or a new beginning. You cannot die how ever much you might want to. If you commit suicide tomorrow you will find you are still alive. Don't mourn for those who "die"; be glad for them, but have lots of compassion for those who are left.

Stop thinking of God as a person, even, as so many of you do, as an old man in the sky. God is neither he nor she, but for the purpose of understanding this work I shall mainly refer to God as He, though sometimes She or even It, for God is another word for Good. We cannot get away from good, for God, good, is in all of us whether we believe it or not. We are all one and all part of God, good. We are not separated by race, religion, colour, age, nation, tribe or anything else. We are all part of the Great Good, the Great Intelligence. There is no one more entitled to being part of good than you. We cannot divide Good any more than we can divide air. IT is everywhere all the time, day and night, North and South. Whether we take advantage of it is up to us.

Rather surprisingly God doesn't punish us for what we do or believe or practise, or whether we pray or not. He already knows everything about us and what is in our hearts at all times. He does not judge because he has given us free will and he says he cannot punish us for going our own way, but he is always there to guide us. This is not to say that it does not matter how we think or behave because this has an effect on others.

Praying is talking to God, good, in our own way. There is no need to implore good for anything, for everything we need and desire is already with us, but most times we cannot see it or believe it. Meditation is listening to God and once you learn to quieten your busy, daily, mortal mind, you will learn to hear God. Your conscience is a good guide; it tells us from childhood what is right and what is wrong for us to be doing, but so many of us choose not to listen to our consciences because we are selfish.

Think of God, good, as a wonderful Friend, one who gives us a grand example and is pleased when we follow it, but does not chastise us when we go "wrong". He, She, It, doesn't accept right or wrong because we have this free choice which we use all the time

4

and only by experience do we learn, or remember, what is best for us.

It is important that we love ourselves otherwise we are not accepting that we are a perfect child of God. When we learn to love ourselves we treat ourselves more kindly and are able to help others more easily. We judge others when we should be loving them, making excuses for what may appear to be their defects, their shortcomings, their characters. Then is the time to give them love, to be understanding, hopefully to be an example of what we feel is better, but always remembering that our way may not be right for them.

* * *

When I wish to 'tune-in' to God I need to make my mind a complete blank. This has taken much practice over the years. Now I am able to attain this by picturing a frame of dove-grey velvet. On this is a beautiful pink rose bud, lying with its head to the right and its stem towards the lower left corner of the frame. There is nothing else in view. This gives me a focal point,. Then I wait.

From now on I shall write my words in italics. The plain print will be what I am hearing, what God is saying, what God is telling me.

— 2000 —

PRAYER

Is prayer any good? How can everyone's prayers be heard?

Dear One, dear Ones, listen with your heart and I will speak to you. I am God, Good, and you are part of me and I am part of you. You are never alone, nor have you ever been. You cannot get away from me for you are made of Me. I know your every thought and aspiration. Your body is a perfect machine which I am running – in spite of all the rubbish you put into it. Your engine is ticking over without you consciously beating your heart or drawing your breaths. You build up difficulties for yourself by interrupting your breathing process with smoke and your thinking process with drugs. You know this, but you do not heed your knowing. I gave you free choice so I condemn you not.

You fear because you have been brought up in fear. Fear of not having enough, fear of not doing well, fear of ridicule, fear of illness, fear of old age and most of all fear of death, which you don't want even to think about. It might seem like asking for trouble to think of death, either for yourself or those you love. Fear that even the simple task of making a Will might bring death nearer. Oh, you silly ones. No, not really for I never condemn I just Love because I am God, Good, All Love. Feel me in your innermost. Don't be afraid of Truth. You can feel this Truth and the more thought you give to what I am conveying the more trust and hope you will experience.

Start your days with affirmations and prayers, no matter how rushed you are, for all you "modern" people live in such a rush. You can give yourself deep thought even under the shower, or while making toast – but don't let it burn!

Do you think you have to be very serious because you are thinking about Me? I am in you and you are in me, we are One and we love each other and the more you love one another the bigger your love grows. As it spreads outwards to all people you can improve every corner of the earth without even going out of your door. You do not have to go into a church or monastery or hall to use your thought. You need not kneel or put your hands together, but if that helps you then do it. In fact your thought is at its best when you are in beautiful surroundings. For some that is open countryside, for others it is woodland or at sea, but really it can be anywhere, for you have the power to create a patch of peace for yourself at any time and in any place, even in a prison.

Can you feel my Love? Try to for it is Great and surrounds you at all times. Your world so needs your love and pure thoughts at this time. You have not found an advanced way of living happily and peacefully. Try not to judge others. So much of that goes on and you will catch yourself doing it, often. You know not why others behave as they do. Give out love to all with whom you come in contact. Jesus said, "offer the other cheek also." Teach your children to listen to their elders and to respect old people, most of whom can give wise counsel. Respect at all ages and for all ages is important. You are all equal and not one of you is better than another or more clever or more loving. You are all equal in the sight of Good, Me, but you have different talents. Encourage yourself and your children and your friends to follow their bent, for they will feel fulfilled by doing what pleases and satisfies them.

Be positive and absorb the Light, the Christ Light as many of you call it. It is the Light of Good. If negative thoughts come up, do not push them away, just let them go through your mind, knowing that they are negative and have no power. All is well now, yes even if you are in pain or distress, all is well, for Life is eternal and you cannot destroy it. You destroy your peace of mind by your actions and thoughts, but you do not destroy the real you, your beautiful you. Love yourself for I made you perfect and you are all different yet all the same. Give out love whether you are driving, shopping, teaching, cooking, reading. That love will get through to what you are doing and will give you pleasure and it will brush off on all and everything with which you come in contact.

Do not try to read this book quickly to reach the end. There is no end and it is better to read a little slowly, than a lot quickly. Open it at random and there will always be a paragraph that meets your needs at that moment. This is so with many books and you will find them or they will come to you as you need them.

HOLDING THE LIGHT

Dear God, I have been asked, "What does it mean to HOLD the LIGHT over places and people?" To me it seems so simple; love is light and light is love and I picture a great 'searchlight' (a six-pointed star) shining down on those of whom I am thinking. Please clarify this.

You need symbols to work with, to focus on. When you write a letter you imagine the items as you relate them, the places, the people, you could not put down words from a black nothingness. So with your spiritual work, you need an image to use as you silently speak your words and listen to my words, in what you call your prayers.

There is also the mortal feeling of space and distance and when praying for others you require a mental picture of places or people on which to concentrate.

When you think of animals, you name them to give you the correct mind-picture otherwise you would not be able to distinguish between a bear and a fox.

It is helpful when you remain quite still when praying. Kneeling or making signs distracts you from your pure thought. You do not require certain clothes or certain movements to speak to me – it doesn't bring you any nearer nor make your prayer more powerful; it is a distraction.

The same questioner asked how I could listen to all of you at once, especially now after that horrific episode in the United States, when so many are praying.

So many of you still think of me, God, as a person. I tell you I am what you call the Great Intelligence, the I Am. I Am in every one of you and you are always connected to me, we are not separate. You do not think of Fear as being limited or of Love being just in some places and limited. Love is everywhere at all times, there to be used, to be enjoyed, to be felt. You do not say there is so much of it in certain places that it cannot get to other places at the same time.

My other name is GOOD; remember that. Good is not limited, rationed, for only certain people, places or species. You can see love amongst animals and birds. You do not think that the love you see in one place cannot be elsewhere. Why do you limit Me?

I keep telling you I am with you always, all ways, everywhere, at all times, in all places, under all circumstances. You cannot get away from me either on earth or at death, in heaven or in India. Do not limit Good, Love, Spirit, Life, because it can weaken your endeavours to help EVERYONE all over your world.

Believe me, your prayers are so important, particularly now, so that Peace may reign, and not destruction. Pray for Peace. Pray for wisdom, for understanding of all peoples, in all places.

God bless you my children – or should I say Good is blessing you now and always.

ETERNAL LIFE

Why are most people so doubtful about their souls? Why do they prefer to believe that this earthly life is the All?

Dear Ones you are surrounded by Love, feel it, breathe it. Why do you doubt your spirit life? You have come from spirit, you will return to spirit. You have done this many times. Some of you remember this; others know this. Have you been to Australia or India? No? Yet you know they exist, you believe what others tell you, you can picture these places, you do not doubt your friends or what you read about these places. Why do you doubt what others tell you about the Heaven World or the World of Spirit? You say there is no proof of these places. I tell you, there is just as much proof as the facts of other continents. Some of you remember this higher life, some of you have returned briefly in what you call a near-death experience. There are many books you can read, there are people you can talk to. You know in your hearts when stories ring true.

If you are satisfied to be just where you are, not interested in anything more, there is nothing wrong with that, but you are not progressing, you are not preparing for your return, for your up-grading. That is not meant in any way to mean you will be better or not better, you are just standing still. You will not be prepared for the wonders of which you remember so little. Know the Truth and The Truth sets you Free. Some of you are so weighed down by cares and worries, pain and grief.

Try to be still within, let peace and love flow through you. Your troubles are temporary illusions which you can shed even before you pass on.

Do some simple tests for yourself. Be still and know that I AM GOD; choose what you desire and know you already have it. Never 'want', for that means you think you have not got it, perhaps cannot have it. You already have everything, so say, many times a day, "I am happy, healthy, wealthy and wise."

Oh, you think 'I am not happy, I am not healthy, I am definitely not wealthy and certainly not wise'. Think again, slowly. A dull or wet day need not make you unhappy, the rain is probably just what your garden or your neighbour needs. If you are grieving for a loved one, know that they are now in a better place, free from pain, be happy for them and call down a blessing on those who are 'left behind'. If you have just been made redundant, know that something else is there for you to do. Open your mind to change and see it as a challenge, a new start.

You think you are unhealthy? Remember all those who cannot walk nor hear nor see. You are breathing, moving, thinking; you have much to be grateful for.

You are not wealthy? You have a roof over your head, you have food, water, warmth, love, clothing, washing facilities. Remember all those who are homeless, starving, without hope. You will feel ashamed to feel unwealthy. Do you really need what is beyond your income? A want isn't always a need. Are those you know with cars, boats, wine, two houses or more, any happier than you?

Then how about wisdom? If you hadn't any of that you would not be reading this book or the many others you are learning from. You can read, you can learn, you can understand. You have wisdom in helping others, tending others, growing your plants, mending your possessions, making artefacts. Think on these things deeply, then repeat, "I am happy, healthy, wealthy and wise." And you know what will happen? In time you will gradually find you have more of these things because you are KNOWING you already have them and there is no short supply.

17.9.00

I choose for you to come through me dear God. May I be worthy and a clear channel for this work at all times. Whatever You choose to put through me will be right for this day and time.

Let us talk about being thankful, being satisfied; about what you can do to help your world and to help each other.

You have just had proof of how powerful thought can be. You have all been feeling unfairly treated because of the price of your fuel, not just in the British Isles, but in countries throughout Europe. Because of thought put into action by a few, that thought was picked up and gathered momentum so fast that your whole country became disrupted in a few days. There were great repercussions until nearly everything came to a standstill. There did not have to be violence nor bad tempers.

Now I am not saying this action was right or wrong, but it certainly had great power. Now you can use this power to improve everything in your world. When enough of you show your feelings, your thoughts, notice has to be taken.

As more and more of you wish for better conditions for your soil, your air, your water, to become more pure, thought will pervade.

Now do this with your thought to all the world. Choose for the starving, the homeless, the terrified to be helped. Pray (which is talking to Me) that these fellow creatures, these loving souls, may experience your happiness, your affluence, your comforts. Choose for enough people to come forward to make it clear that this is what you desire. Choose for the rich to give to the poor. Do not be afraid that by doing so you will become poorer. For I tell you this, you will all become richer and happier.

Choose for those among you who are able, to go forth and communicate with these people, without fear. Some do that already. Fear not to mix among the starving, the diseased. Choose for your great love to reach them. Not, as in earlier days, when men went forth trying to teach them that there is a God to fear, who would judge them if they didn't live as those teachers thought they should. Men went out to them, then when they responded others stepped in and persecuted them, enslaved them, used them for their own selfish ends. Let those who go forth now expect nothing in return. Let them show their brothers in distress how to have hope, how to look after themselves. Let them see, by example, what unselfish love is.

Let all the rich give to the poor. Let all nations cease making armaments and training armies to fight one another. Choose for men to live satisfied in the position they are in. Choose for mankind to be satisfied to stay on their own "patch" of the world. Why should they want to take my land away from others, for, as I have explained earlier, by wanting they will never obtain anything. If you have a coat, and most of you have several, why would you want to take another's.

If you live by love instead of money all your needs will be met. I will keep telling you this. Be thankful for all that you have. I will repeat these talks, because it is taking centuries for the Truth to reach you, my children. Through fear you are afraid to put my teaching into practice. Little children are afraid to take their first step; you are very little children.

Thank you dear God for this lesson. May it be one of very many and may these teachings reach out to many, many people.

THE POWER OF LOVE

May I have some more teaching for those I think of as in their 'middle ages'? I feel that group is the most interested in learning more.

Just picture that dove grey velvet and pink rose-bud which seems to bring you peace and quiet.

Dear Ones, be still and know that you are listening to me, Good, who is also YOU. You are good, for you are part of Me; your thought is my thought and my thought is your thought. I am not speaking of all the chatter that goes on both verbally and mentally, but of the deeper thoughts that come to you. Seek and choose to know more, for all truth is within you and around you. Look for beauty, listen for knowledge, choose to feel love – love for all creatures. Call your dog or cat to you if you have one and sit quietly stroking it and feel and give that love between you. Your pets pick up your feelings so easily. Look into their eyes and see into their souls; give out love to them and they will adore you for it. Have you ever known your pet push you away when you have been loving it? Love feeds them like it feeds you. Even the birds in the trees respond to your attunement with them.

When you give out love it goes forth in ripples that reach so much further than you realise, comforting, up-lifting, strengthening those around you and those of whom you are thinking, however far away they are, for there is no space. There is no space between us now. I am wrapping you around with love and you can feel it and I can feel what is in your heart, meaning your truth, your integrity. I love you and you must learn to love yourself for you are beautiful, perfect, all love.

You may be suffering from pain, either physically or mentally or emotionally, but I am with you; I never leave you; you can bear your seeming pain for it is transitory, even although you may not think so. Rise above all sorrow, all pain, all anxiety. Do not let others pull you down with their negative thoughts. Do not enter into arguments, just pour out love to everything, everyone. You will see and feel what that does, for it will not only comfort you, but it will help them. They may appear to be much better than you; better healthwise, moneywise, intellectually, but that means you are judging them. You know not what is going through their minds.

Sometimes others try to influence you to do what they wish, but that may not be what you wish for yourself. That is when you must not be afraid to be firm, to be strong. Do not be aggressive nor argumentative, just be calm and use your own thoughts of love. You know others cannot argue with you if you do not argue back. They give up trying to persuade you against your will and the calmer you are the more difficult it is for them to try to influence you.

Now I am not suggesting you be 'difficult' or obstinate or narrow-minded. Oh, no. That will get you nowhere. Try to see another's point of view. Be willing to change your mind or alter your outlook, but be firm when you are using your powers of love and knowledge and instinct. You can look upon instinct as a prod from me, Good, to remind you to do this thinking, but I will never use persuasion – only love.

When you start to realise and feel how strong love is in all circumstances you will be amazed at the results you achieve and the example you set. Others will be drawn to you. They will listen to you, so be very thoughtful what you say and never use your own mortal will on others.

If you are asked for guidance, tune in to your higher self and pray (ask Me) how best you can help your brother man. You know that 'man' means humankind, woman, people. You have become so taken up with racism, sexism, when none is there.

Oh, dear ones, you look for trouble instead of good and peace. Words are just words, they are not feelings. Certain words you choose to call swear words, dirty words, obscenities, but they are really just sounds uttered by your voice mechanism and any one word could be chosen to be objectionable, even the word Love if enough people started calling it obscene. Some of you when annoyed use simple words like sugar, socks or blast, yet they are ordinary words. It is the ability of being able to swear as you call it that eases the situation in which you sometimes find yourselves. The voicing of a word relieves your feelings at that moment, it is a kind of mental smack to yourself or another and is really harmless is it not?

I leave you now with all love, all understanding, all peace. Peace, Peace.

DOUBT

Dear God, Good, please come through me that I may know I am truly doing your work for the good of the planet which is being so sorely abused by humankind. I clear my mind of clutter and listen for you to impress me with the truth. Sometimes it has seemed so remarkably easy that I am afraid I imagine your words and am just using mine.

Have I not said TRUST, many times. You are a Resource and we do not waste our resources, like you on earth do. We need the help of all loving souls who wish to be used.

Your words, which are also mine, will be used. Nothing, no thing, that is good is wasted.

Can you feel my love, for it is great and deep?

Yes, my child of course I can feel your love and it is deep and sincere. Your love comforts me as mine comforts you. Think about that. There is no separation in Love. There is no separation between you and me, you and your higher self, the real you. When you 'work' for others as you do most days, you are tuning in to Good and that Light goes out to them in great waves. Never doubt your spiritual work is wasted or not used. It goes on and on being used and the volts jolt through it every time you tune in.

You, my child, feel much love for all things, not only your friends and neighbours, but for your surroundings. Think of that love rippling across the countryside that you love, it is blessing the soil, the seeds, the wild life. And it comes back to you as a blessing from Me, God. You cannot get away from me. Trust me with your 'patients', your family, your civilised own well-being. Cast out all fears. You will never want unless you tell yourself that you are without and wanting. You have all you need, for you have all Love at all times.

Sow seeds of thankfulness to those around you by what you say and convey. Bless them, as you often do, knowing that that blessing reaches into their souls and gives them a glow.

Concentrate for longer on your work for the planet. The more of you who pray for your planet the better, for it is in a sorry state at this time. Wars, fighting, squabbling, are rife. Your earth is rumbling with anger at the way it has been treated. Greed abounds in all 'civilised' countries. Though how you can call them civilised is surprising. So much has to be learned, remembered.

Children, my children, you do not try to see the glory that is yours already. You are afraid to let go of your petty power. You want more and more. You do not have the pleasure of appreciating what you already have – which is all you need. You can be so happy with so little if only you would understand that. You have forgotten how to live joyfully.

As soon as a nation is brave enough to say "No more armaments, no more fighting, no more armies, no more harmful chemicals. We will lead the way", oh, how powerful, not weak, that would be. Other nations would look on astounded. They would be too astonished to invade. They would hold back in awe, in wonder, that that nation had the strength to be so brave.

The people, especially the women, of other nations would rise up and implore their governments to do the same thing. Fear would fly out of their boundaries, their souls, and they would know the beginning of real Peace, real Love, real brotherhood. It will come, but it is up to all of you how soon it comes and where it starts.

Many who think themselves so wise and disagree will try to stand firm to their old beliefs, but they will find Good prevailing without any violence.

Women can play a big part in this change. Women more easily learn compassion, need less of what you call power; yet the power of Good is mighty and overcomes all. Pray for world peace. Pray deeply and sincerely and fearlessly and the more you pray the sooner you will know heaven on earth.

Thank you dear God.

* * *

To my readers:

I had been hoping that I am getting through to you just how easy and simple it is for you to 'get through to Good' and how easy to believe in Good. Then I hear some sceptic on the media stating they have no faith, there is nothing beyond this life, we are deluded when we think there is anything else. They usually wear a belligerent expression and I know nothing I could say to them would cut any ice.

How sad this is. Why do so many people, intelligent, well-educated people, prefer to think this way? It cannot give them satisfaction surely. Wouldn't you prefer to believe that tomorrow is going to be a good, healthy, happy day for you than to declare that you will be ill, depressed, soaked through with rain, utterly alone with no friends?

You cannot see your lungs, your heart, your intestines, but they are all there doing miraculous work and keeping you alive. You do not have to argue or wonder about them. You accept the fact. You take it for granted that your organs will know how to continue working. If they do go wrong you usually consult a doctor and listen to what he says, what she explains, and you probably take some remedies.

I wonder why you have to doubt your Being. You cannot see your soul, spirit, love, intelligence, sadness, joy, memory, but you know all but the first two are there. It is those first two you doubt. What are they? They are the most important part of your Goodness, your Being, your connectedness.

If you wish to test your lungs you can take a conscious deep breath or two and feel them working. If you want to be conscious of your heart, run hard, or hurry upstairs, and notice how your heartbeat has increased. If you want to feel love hug your pet or your partner or your parent and feel that very enjoyable something within your heart centre. If you want to test your memory think back to a particular group of people or places and see how many names you can recall. All these things are easy for you. Yes?

But how, you wonder, can you really tune in to Good, another name for God. First you put up a big barrier by thinking it is impossible, you are not worthy, there is nothing there or it would just be your imagination playing tricks with you.

Only have a little bit of faith. You cannot suffer harm by doing it. Do you remember your first stroke alone at swimming or your first wobbly cycle ride? You were afraid you would sink or fall. Then it suddenly became so easy you wondered why you had been so afraid.

Take my hand now, it is warm and loving, it will not let go of you. Empty your mind and form a beautiful, tranquil scene. Keep very still and positive. Know you are going to experience the most rewarding occurrence that ever happened to you.

KNOW YOU ARE PART OF GOOD, GOD. Realise that you are never alone. Feel joined to everyone else and every living creature. Look at the view and see that there are no spaces.

You are important, you are part of an eternal chain, an on-going mass; an eventuality of the past and a necessity of the future. BUT there is no past nor future, all is now. You are just as important to God as that tiny ant or that wonderful sunset. Be very still and know you are alive and eternal. Do this often until it becomes so easy. Then dare to listen.

* * *

HELP IS AT HAND

My child, my beloved child, I am here. I am with you always. I guide you when you will let me, as you are now, but I never force you. You have free choice at all times. That is why I never condemn you. It is my wish that you experience the full beauty of your Being. Come to me in the silence of your mortal mind and tell me of your troubles, your joys, your hopes. I already know them, but it is good for you to talk to me, to make contact.

I am ALL GOOD, but I am only all good. Think about that. You have no need to feel in awe, unworthy, afraid. I am no monster; I am your loving guardian. I AM GOOD, WHICH BY CALLING ME GOD, YOU HAVE MADE ME SEEM LIKE A PERSON. I tell you I am good and you are made of me. You can experience all I experience. I experience me through you and you experience you through me. Think deeply about this. Do not rush through these talks. Listen, learn and remember. All this is already in your soul.

I will tell you something. This writer has just pressed a wrong button and her work became interrupted, her connection with me temporarily

17

broken. She tried to find the solution to her error, but failed. So she telephoned someone who would be able to help her. She almost panicked, but she 'saved' her work up to that point. The remedy was simple.

This helped her for our next 'lesson'. You often need human help and there is always someone who knows more than you do. So ask them. Nothing was lost. She is back on our wave-length. She didn't ask me for that help – she knew she must ask another human being. I am not with you to tell you which button to press, but to guide you on occasion to another who is further along your path. I will guide you to that person. Then this writer guided herself back to me. She chose to carry on with what I was guiding her to write.

Choice in all things is yours. Choose to learn or remember or give help. Choose to meet people who think along your lines, for you will learn from each other. Choose to find the books that will best help you at the stage at which you have arrived.

You would not choose to take a plane to a town ten miles away, nor a taxi to a remote island. Of course not, you are thinking. Don't be ridiculous. I tell you, you do do some ridiculous things! You do think some ridiculous things. You do fear some ridiculous things.

Start each day with hope, optimism, love, patience with yourself and with others. Smile, oh, do smile. You become so beautiful when you smile. Keep knowing that all is well now, how ever bad things seem to you, for it is only a seeming, not a reality. If you put your baby in a stiff net ball you would know that however much that ball turned and twisted, tossed in the air, went through a storm, that baby could not fall out. Do not make a hole in the ball and expect it to work the same as before.

Think about your world in this way. You have made a hole and wrong influences are pouring in and pouring out. That hole has to be repaired and it will take all thinking people to mend that hole. There is not much earthly time left to do this. The hole is getting bigger and bigger each day. Choose to mend it.

I am in that wonderful shaft of brilliant white light; it comes down like a searchlight and envelopes me. It makes me feel very safe. It is like being wrapped in white silk; it is soft and warm and it is all love.

I am ready to receive knowledge. I "await the incoming of the Light" as it states in one of the White Eagle books.

You and I are close, you know that, but I am no closer to you than I am to all my children, though all of them do not want to know. You have a saying "you can lead a horse to water, but you cannot make it drink". When the horse is thirsty it will drink greedily.

Most of your time, all of you, you are so busy-busy, you do not stop to listen to your higher mind, your connection with Me.

Mankind needs to find an alternative way of living which does not waste your planet's resources. There are ways and there are plenty of souls on this side ready to implant this knowledge into receptive minds.

Some of your so-called scientists are so cock-sure of themselves, they do not listen to their inner-knowing which is trying to guide them into better ways of living. You are riding roughshod over your planet instead of treading gently, with love and kindness to your earth. You would not plant a rose tree, anticipating beautiful blooms, then when they were about to open cut them all off. Good has given you all you need to survive and to live in peace and happiness, but the few spoil it for the many.

Although I say fear is one of your enemies, I would suggest you do fear what you are doing to your planet. You are using up its resources willy-nilly, without thought for tomorrow. Can you not be satisfied with the beauty of what is there for you all to enjoy. The 'primitive' peoples as you call them, can be happy with so little when they are left to their own devices. They do not need 'civilised' man to try to alter their ways. He marches in, thinking he knows better. I tell you most times he does not.

Concentrate on your own countries, grow your own food, seek different means of heating and travelling; study the simple healing properties of your wild plants, for they were put there for a purpose for your own particular needs in your part of your planet. Read "The Last Hours of Ancient Sunlight" which I guided Thom Hartmann to write.

Good has power and overcomes so-called evil. Evil is greed with a capital G. You want, want, want, but I tell you you do not Need a quarter of what you want.

You can learn much from the ancient North American Indian way of life. They were peaceful, grateful, quiet. They called down the blessing of Good on their crops and that did much more good than chemicals. They revered the earth and its bounty. They were happy because they were peaceful and satisfied. When you eat a good meal you feel satisfied, you do not wish for more. When you are warm you do not wish to be hotter, when you are truly happy you do not wish to be happier for you feel satisfied.

Some of you are thinking all this sounds boring, not exciting enough for you. That is because you are ever seeking, but not finding what your soul desires. You make so much noise we cannot get near you. When you are truly in love you do not rant and rave at your loved one with loud noise to make your point, you use gentleness and soft words. Oh, that you could experience this true feeling of peace. It is so true that perfect Peace casts out fear, it feeds the soul, it satisfies all your needs.

Be still and know that I Am God, Good, talking to you through this medium. She 'aches' to pass on to you my words and her own feeling of Peace. She has learned to experience this through much striving. She knows nothing, no thing, can take away from her all that matters most in her life and she has no fear of 'dying'. She is truly looking forward to her next experience.

Put yourself in this ray of white light. When you are concerned about loved ones try putting them in this ray of protective light. It works, it is mighty, it is beyond your grasping, yet it is within your grasp. Pray, talk to me; then listen and you will hear my words guiding you if you are truly seeking. Open your bible (if you have one!) at the New Testament and pick out some of that beloved Master Jesus's sayings. Take them in. You need not try to understand any parts that seem difficult. The 'right' passages will stand out for you to absorb.

Try to let others know what you are endeavouring to learn about a better way of living. But do not go to extremes by shouting it from the roof tops, for that frightens people off. Be gentle in all things, especially with your children. They need your guidance, your example, your true love and patience, your care. Hold them in this white light of protection. Communicate with them at their own level, communicate instead of sitting them in front of your television to keep them quiet because you haven't the time or patience to communicate with them yourself. It is never too early to do this; at first it is just by letting them feel your love, then soon it is by your words and your example. Everything you do is taken in by your children and stored in their minds. You do not want to fill their larders with food that will go bad, that will deteriorate, but with pure food that will withstand the conditions with which they will come into contact.

That is enough for you to absorb for the moment and my writer is losing clear contact because she wants to read what she has just written!

God bless you my beloved children. I love you.

WAR & PEACE

11.11.00

I have just been greatly helped by re-listening to tapes by Raj through Paul Tuttle.* Yes, it really is easy to communicate with you dear God. In a way it is easier than hoping to communicate with Raj, because you are no longer a person to me, just perfect Good. I feel that communication with Raj belongs to Paul. What do you wish me to write today?

Today is the day you call Armistice Day, Remembrance Day, when thousands of you give thanks for the lives of those that made it possible for your country to have Peace once again. During that two-minute silence a great wave of Good Thought, Love and Peace ascends from your planet and we all feel your thoughts. Even the children that take part, though they never endured war, feel that atmosphere that you create from your hearts. You all partake of that precious moment of stillness, thinking your own thoughts.

It is painful for many of you to listen to or watch the media re-living that horror. It is helpful for the younger generations to see and hear what was experienced, that they may better know the futility and devastation of war amongst nations. It is so important that you all learn to live together in peace, judging no man, no nation, but in trying to understand how situations arise. Usually the cause is Greed.

There is great strength in right thoughts, peaceful thoughts, loving thoughts. As more and more of you are realising the necessity of altering

---

* NWFFACIM
P.O. Box 1490
Kingston, WA 98346-1490
USA

your ways of living, there is a shift towards peace. You are at the beginning of the Golden Age, as it has been referred to, when there will be no more wars and peace will reign throughout the land. Can you imagine how different you, all peoples, will feel when you have no fear of other nations, bombs, nuclear weapons?

At this time you dread, deep within you, the possibility of annihilation, tremendous storms, floods. But you will feel a great surge of a peace you have never experienced. At this moment many of you in this land are suffering from floods and the rest of you feel helpless to help those sufferers.

The best help you can give to all peoples is to know that you can alter your climate back to the beautiful one it used to be. It is in your hands, not Mine. You need to heed the warnings.

You need to think deeply about not eating your brother animals. Some of you will now stop doing this through fear of disease, but it would be better were you to stop through compassion. You would not eat your dog or your cat, yet you kill those docile animals that have trusted you – the cows, the sheep, the pigs, the birds. These are easy prey, but when it is more difficult you take a gun to them, sometimes only maiming them and leaving them to suffer the remainder of their lives.

I tell you, it is not necessary to kill your fellow creatures. I have given you all you need for your sustenance and many of you know this. Even those who now make a living through the slaughter of animals know this, but they fear for their livelihoods. There will always be work for you, a means of making a living as you call it. You are trying to get quicker and quicker, wealthier and wealthier, what you think is clever and cleverer. And what is happening? Your world is full of stress, famine, drought, floods, catastrophes.

Pray for true Peace, real knowledge. Let go of fear. Calm down. Stop what you call the Rat Race for it is getting you nowhere, except towards destruction.

I have said before, prayer is mighty and the more of you who pray for a better world the sooner it will come about.

Trust, Pray and Love more, my children. I am with you always, guiding you into ways of Peace.

13.11.00

I am encouraged today by hearing that two important meetings are taking place to do with global warming, one of those meetings involving several countries. It seems that suddenly more thinking people are questioning what has to be done to stop pollution. Can you intimate to me, dear God, how effective these meetings will be and how soon our scientists will 'discover' alternative means of transport and heating?

Mankind is on the verge of a big, necessary leap forward in these vital subjects.

Starting to heal your planet will not only improve your atmosphere, but it will improve the health of you, my people.

All knowledge is within your scientists already, but they will be up against much opposition when they bring it forth for it will affect many big money-makers.

Greed rears its ugly head here, for those who are made rich by worldly standards will be afraid of giving up their pursuits. What will be 'discovered' will be mainly free to all. There are resources available that do not require digging and burning and building. There is a Source that is free, just as Love is free, daylight is free, thinking is free.

You think you made wonderful progress in the last century with your discoveries, especially in the field of communication, but I tell you, all that is as nothing to what will be achieved in this century. It will be a revelation to all people.

You can all help in bringing this about by your deep wish, your sincere hope, that you wish to take part in this revelation. To do that you need to become deeply peaceful, then hold your planet in the White Light of my Love and Direction to you. Pray, (tell me) that you wish to become more knowledgeable in improving your planet for the sake of all people, not just the few, but all people of all countries. This way you can begin to set in action the coming of the Golden Age.

The simple elements are already there for your use, both for travel and for warmth and light. These natural elements, as yet unused in your memory of Time, will not dissipate nor pollute your lives and your countries. It will be a discovery free to all my people of all races and in all parts of the globe.

Mankind needs to open its mind to the possibility of Divine Guidance. It is a case of knock, ask and enter. Humility will not be amiss . The way is simple, as with most Truth, but man makes conditions complicated when he tries so hard to be 'clever'. Try being humble, try simple prayer, then listen for the answers which are awaiting the listening Minds.

Your preachers and your teachers would do well to ask for divine guidance here. Your true requests never go unanswered. The many can overcome the few, in Peace. Always in Peace.

I, God, Good, am in each one of you. I will keep telling you that. Use me. That is what I am here for. I do not desire worship nor awe. I am here to give you Love and I am here to accept your Love. We will talk about this many times. I tell you nothing, no thing, is beyond your comprehension, especially when it is for the good of all.

Be positive in all your thinking; expect Good to come and it will. It is so simple, but you do not see it. Pray and listen, pray and listen, many times a day.

God bless you all, my beloved children.

19.11.00

I await the incoming of the Light, God's message to me this day.

Nothing, except pictures of sand, desert. miles of it. Then compressed sand, being made into tiny blocks, the size of postage stamps and about $^1/_4$" thick. Why? Could this become a form of energy? Sand, sand, miles of it in Africa, Australia. Nothing else today.

20.11.00

I feel compelled to try this writing every day and it is becoming increasingly easy to make my mind a blank.

I have told you I am always here. Use me.

I am grateful for being able to say 'thank you' night and morning, and many times a day, for all my blessings and the warm feeling of knowing you, dear God, are always so close. I do not feel full of questions to ask you. Currently I am so concerned with what we are doing to our world. I am disappointed how few people really seem to want to do anything about it. There is such a response of "I'm all right, Jack", which I find disturbing.

World leaders at last seem to be realising something urgent has to be done about global warming and the using up of our resources. Surely now is the time for alternative energy to be 'discovered', for even when discovered it is going to take so long, in my humble opinion, for it to be accepted. Mankind has made such an Idol and necessity of having wealth, far more wealth than is appropriate.

REMUNERATION

Why should heads of great companies expect to earn so much more than our doctors, scientists, ordinary workmen – workmen who often do long hours far above their employers; nurses so dedicated to their work that they do not count time?

This is where humankind has made a backward step in using money, especially as a status symbol. For those who 'discover', 'invent', act, lead, teach, all these attributes are a privilege. These talents are a joy because they enable the recipient to give joy to others. Then the receivers, full of gratitude, can find joy in giving of their wares, their labour, their thoughtfulness in appreciation for what they have received.

Do you begin to understand this. Nothing, no thing, has any monetary value. You do not try to pay me. Why? Because you know I have all, and money would be of no use to me, would it? Then try to understand that because you are part of me, you also already have everything you need and money is not appropriate.

There are little groups of people around the country who have started to live by giving to others of their wares and accepting wares or labour in exchange. When nothing is required by the recipient at that moment, there is a points system so that recipient can receive 'repayment' at a future date. These points are a kind of IOU and that is how money came into being in the first place.

When it comes to immense amounts of goods, there can be immense amounts of points. There will always be those who are willing 'to get their hands dirty' and those who are too weak to do heavy jobs, but that does not stop the system working.

25

You think 'how could that work over really big developments, like laying roads, building buses, etc.', but give this deep thought. When you have learned how to move without trains, cars, planes, you will not need to make such giant commodities. And there is no need to build great edifices to me in the way of enormous cathedrals and mosques. It doesn't help your prayers to reach me any quicker than in your minds; in fact it takes much longer. And how would I pay you? Well, just as I do now, with love and guidance and the gift of all you really need.

In a way, money enables you to have what you have not earned. You are a long way yet from Utopia my children, but it will come. Many of you know the joy of giving your own produce in return for a neighbour mending your shed or comforting you in the loss of a dear one. There is no price on anything worthwhile. If you have a wondrous voice, give pleasure to others by singing to them, free, and all doors will be open to you all over the world to feed and sleep you for nothing but appreciation.

Yes, you think that is all right for those with exceptional talent, but I tell you, you all have exceptional talent, from sharpening knives to growing carrots, from designing a house to healing a pet. Is one talent really worth more than another?

Learn to give, give, give of yourself and learn also to be gracious in accepting. That is important. Be gracious.

By living this way you are really able to be happy, healthy, wealthy and wise. You will be happy inside, in your soul which is the real you, because you are selflessly giving and warmly accepting; healthy because greed, jealousy, envy and fear are leaving your thoughts; wealthy because you realise there is nothing you wish for is now impossible, and wise because you are learning to live how I hoped you would live – that is in harmony with all things, all people, all nature.

Incidentally do you picture, those of you who do picture, your next life, using money? Have you ever thought you would need to use money in 'heaven'? You would not expect to say to me, or Jesus or Moses, "Here is £10, please can I have a bowl of fruit."

Your minds are so powerful you do not use a tenth of their strength, yet it is there, freely to be used in your present life on your earth plane. If there were no money, would there be crime, do you think? If there were no money would there be rich and poor? If there were no money you would be able to choose your favourite book in hardback instead of paperback. A bunch of parsley would be equal to a bundle of asparagus. Do you see how you would be getting things in proportion?

Would you breed dogs, at the expense of causing them to be deaf or with breathing problems, if they were of no more value than what you call a mongrel? Would you race horses, whipping them almost beyond their endurance, instead of riding them in the countryside for sheer pleasure?

There is nothing wrong with competition for the joy of winning a game, an achievement, so long as the prize is not money. Your prize could be the privilege of teaching others how you won or achieved.

You would experience leisure and freedom instead of frustration and stress. You would not be afraid that another's discovery would take away your livelihood. It would probably only make it easier.

Think on these things, my children. Think long and hard. Pray often. My love is with you.

COMMUNICATING WITH GOD

How long will this work that I am doing go on? How will I get it to others for their benefit?

This work, this project, as you call it, will never cease. It will go on and on, for everyone can do it. When you wish to stop you can stop. It is up to you.

I can't imagine ever wanting to stop; it gets easier and more wondrous to me.

As I said to you yesterday, you can pass on your way of working to others; they can benefit from it, not only by listening but by doing what you do. You have started another ball rolling, just as Neale Donald Walsch did with his trilogy, "Conversations with God". And without his work you might not be doing this now. There is no end, for it is in your nature, all of you, to want to learn about your life, your everlasting life.

You, yourself, are feeling nearer to your 'dead' loved ones than ever before. You do not try to communicate with them for I know you do not feel that is your work, but you are conscious of them being just as much alive as when you knew them on your earth.

You are realising how thin the veil is between you and them. You feel their aura, you feel connected to them; you feel their love.

LIFE AFTER DEATH (I)

Am I right to feel so strongly about not trying to prolong life here, about not accepting organ transplants, even blood transfusions?

You feel this way because you do not fear death and because you wish to have only your own organs and your own blood. You do not want what you consider is God's work interfered with.

There are others who feel urged to try to interfere with my work. This applies to bodies, plants, animals, insects, and so on. You all have free choice and you also have the capacity to influence others in your way of thinking. Much of it is done in what would be called 'your best interests', but some is done for greed – that old choice, GREED.

I asked you yesterday, have you ever considered there may be those who think they could use money in 'heaven'. Well, do you, some of you, think 'transplants' will be carried out in your next phase of life? If not, it is because you know, deep down, the next phase is so different. You do not anticipate being ill, being blind, being broke, being cold. No? Why? Because you anticipate being much nearer to perfection in your next state.

The way you think will still affect your next life, but your willingness to change your minds about things will alter. You will find that thought is so powerful. Thought manifests instantaneously. You will read, learn and listen with your minds, but there will not be the delay between thought and action. Thought is action, is instantaneous.

I know you, yourself, expect your 'death' to be an instantaneous shift into another dimension, and so it will be. There are those who think there is a long wait before they 'wake up'; there are those who expect nothing. You will experience what you expect, until you change your expectations after your earthly life. There is no time so it does not matter if you wish to take a long time to 'wake up'.

You, my child, will want to be everywhere at once; seeing all the beauty, the gardens, the halls of learning. You will expect to see all your friends and relations quickly, all at once. Yes, you are smiling because I read your mortal mind so well.

There are others who will take situations slowly, one at a time. For some it is going to be a shock to find themselves alive. They will need to do much different thinking.

Some of you, most of you, will experience real Peace for the first time. You will bask in peace, bliss. Your earth life will seem much, much less important from this new angle. You will soon forget all those material things that meant so much to some 'earthlings'. They cling on to them 'like grim death' while on earth. You notice how you call death grim, horrific, devastating, tragic. Yes, it seems like that to those who are left behind, but do not mourn for those who go on. They just want you on earth to know what joy awaits you.

The actual moment of death, that is when your soul, your spirit, leaves your body, is instantaneous. It is no more than going to sleep and waking up. You are not conscious of either actual moment. But instead of waking up to your familiar surroundings, you awake to a different 'atmosphere', a new vibration, but it will seem very like the one you have been accustomed to.

I cannot tell you too often, there is nothing to fear.

So much of what you call 'time' is wasted in fear and worry. It achieves nothing. It is destructive. It is useless. Better by far to hope, love, understand, breathe in my love. It is ever around you, my beloved children. My blessing to you all. It is always there for you to absorb.

FEELING EMOTIONS

My two favourite hymns have been haunting me the last few days. I rather dreaded having to listen to them at the White Eagle Lodge services because I could not keep the tears back, they affected me so deeply.

These hymns are "May God's blessing be with you this day (night)" and "Make me a Channel for Thy Peace". Well, these requests have come true. Sometimes I want to change the word Peace for Light and sometimes for Love. And these melodies still bring tears. I feel so very blessed. Why do some tunes make us weep?

While you are on the earth plane, there is only so much that you can bear with equanimity. Think of a long straight road. You travel along it, knowing you can see ahead and are prepared to act appropriately. You can keep this up easily. Then there is a curve and you do not know what is round the corner. Now, most times, you can cope with it, but sometimes you experience a shock and if it is a bad accident that you witness it makes you feel what you call bad or sick. Now if, on the other hand, you behold a wonderful sunset or a marvellous view you experience a different deep emotion.

This does not happen to everyone; it depends on your capacity of feeling. Can you understand you have edged off that straight road you thought you were on and either slipped into the ditch or reached the brow of a hill where the view is what you call breath-taking. This deep encounter is a shock to your normal way of feeling. You could say your very soul has been affected by the unexpected. Your equilibrium has been jolted.

Going back to your feeling about certain music, it has that same effect, it touches deep within, it strikes a chord you could say, that resonates your very Being and your joy spills over. Remember there are tears of happiness as well as tears of sorrow.

There is only a certain amount of sorrow or joy or pain you can bear while in your earthly bodies. You know it is said you are never given more than you can bear, that is why you faint when pain becomes too much to bear.

There is nothing to be ashamed of in showing your feelings, experiencing your feelings; it can be a taste of greater things to come when you are on a higher vibration.

Just as a child, especially a very young child, soon laughs or cries when you do not, so it is with you. Do you understand what I am trying to tell you?

Yes, I am picturing what you are saying. Is it harder for a person to get over the loss of a loved one when they have no faith?

There is not a definite yes or no to that question. But I would say it may be easier because, without faith or much deep thought, there is also not the same extent of being affected by what we have been talking about. Does that answer your question?

Yes, I think so, I will know better when I read this through. Thank you.

RAISING CHILDREN

Something that is concerning me at present is the terrible lack of self control and discipline amongst the young teenagers, especially the boys. Where are we going so sadly wrong in their upbringing?

There is such a lack of love for many of the children. Their parents find little joy in their upbringing. Children need love and discipline, in that order. You do not shove a tiny seed into rough ground and expect it to grow healthily. One little flower, if it does flower, would look, and does look, very pathetic all alone with none of its kind around it. If it is taken up, replanted with love and care, fed and watered, it thrives and repays with beauty, be it only a weed. Why should children starved of real affection and understanding grow up displaying gentleness, love, thoughtfulness, unselfishness? Has it been shown those attributes by those adults around it? Instead it feels compelled to protect itself, defend itself, learn to cope by any means. Put several like-minded young ones together and they try to outdo one another and, worse still, to outdo and over power those who show authority over them or try to discipline them.

A child that has not been disciplined at home, enters school with mixed feelings of fear, resentment and lack of confidence. As soon as it is shown or told what to do its reaction is too often one of resentment. If it had been told lovingly beforehand that it would have to conform to certain rules for the sake of the many, and do what it is told as at home, its whole attitude is open instead of closed.

Your schools would find it so much easier to teach young ones if they would start right from the beginning to teach the need for compliance. Teach your children both at home and at school to choose to be happy, choose to be kind, choose to be giving. Let this attitude run through all lessons so that it becomes an expected experience.

Remember your own attitude, your own aura, is all around you, brushing off on those close to you, be it at home or in a class. Why are some teachers so much more effective than others, why are some more respected than others? Children soon pick up the atmosphere around them. A happy child will learn fast, especially with a lot of encouragement. Do you see how important that early example is? Go about it the wrong way and you sow seeds of discontent, lack of respect and much resentment. Encourage youngsters to have hobbies; that way they discover what they can do better than other things. All of you are different and all of you do some things better than others. That way life is more interesting for you.

As teachers, I would say to you, expect good, expect respect, expect love even from what you might describe as the toughest children. Try to understand their resentment, hold them in the Light of Love, try it, it works. Children are rarely too young to learn about their souls, their personalities, their usefulness. Tell them how to be happy, that happiness is found in helping others, not in bullying them or belittling them. You know yourself how good it makes you feel when you receive praise for your kindness or thoughtfulness. I cannot stress too often the importance of giving out love and patience.

Thugs and bullies are not happy, they just don't know how to be different, nor the pleasure they could experience. They do not need a pompous, self-righteous person to come to talk to them about sin, fear of God, possible hell, no entrance into a better life without penance. No, they need, often, to be taught how to be happy, loved, respected; how to help others to be happier; how to help at home, willingly, even when not asked to do anything. You, you, you, make these youngsters what they are or become. If you want your prisons to diminish, start now to alter those within your field of remit by your outlook, your example, your understanding. There is not time to waste if you want a more peaceful world.

Know that a better world is coming and you can be instrumental in making it happen sooner rather than later.

POWERFUL FORCES

This tuning-in is becoming so simple to me, I just expect to hear your messages. I never wish to get used to this marvellous privilege. I do not think I shall because there is ever this tiny doubt that I might be imagining all this. It is when I read through what I have typed that I realise it is not the little me writing. Mostly, I never know what the subject is going to be, nor even what questions I will ask.

I have been watching many wonderful documentaries lately about volcanoes, earthquakes, whirlpools, tornados, hurricanes, let alone the wonders of wild animal life. How little we know. How mighty is the force of what we call nature. I do wonder why the earth has to be so awesome. Are there other planets very like this one, or are they mostly all calmer and more gentle?

You understand what perspective is. Just picture an ant or a little beetle in your garden. What must it seem like to them when one big rain drop falls on them, or a hailstone. They find cover from deep snow or frost; shelter from a breeze, or extreme heat. They have the capacity of self preservation. You look on and think little about raindrops or snowflakes or thunder and lightning. You do not fear what you are used to. What to those creatures is so big, is so small to you.

This is a difficult question for you to have answered to your satisfaction. This is mainly because fear of the unknown or unexperienced is there. Those tiny beings are not unduly frightened. You are not unduly frightened while you only have to look on and not experience what you see.

I tell you Thought, Love and Belief are as mighty as these phenomena you have been speaking of. Think about that. Thought is so much mightier than you can possibly understand until you put it into practice.

Energy is everywhere. If ants could see your energy, your power, your thought, they would be terrified, but they just accept their life at this moment. When you can understand that energy, that power, you will think differently. Those who go to photograph those eruptions and storms have less fear than others and that enables them to get close to what would terrify most of you.

Now adjust this to you, yourself, your own lack of fear of death. You know there is nothing to fear. You do not dread its approach. You know there is nothing to fear, yet there are thousands who dread death. It is more terrifying to them than the sight of those great global manifestations. You can use your self, your understanding, to help others and that is mainly why you do this work. You are so sorry for people who fear, just as a good swimmer would be sorry for you when he felt your fear of deep water.

You will be used, you are being used, to help others. Just as you keep opening books and finding answers and subjects that are just right for you at that moment, so you will be used at the right moments in the lives of others. I have told you, we do not waste our resources!

You will be guided so long as you keep open this contact, so long as you wish to do this work, so long as you stop doubting, so long as you want to be useful. Bless you my child.

GUIDES & GUIDANCE

When I first experienced teachings and 'information' coming through me, I guessed it was through my Guide. Now I feel I have by-passed my Guide and am in direct contact with you, dear God. Will you please explain.

All of you have Guides, though most of you are not conscious of the fact. At first, when you get inquisitive, you try out contacting your Guide. You play a little secretive game with a thought or a question to see if anything happens. When it seems to, you wonder if you are just imagining it. Well you are really imagining a contact because you need to use your imagination. When you think of a garden full of flowers, you imagine all the plants, trees, colours, scents – you are imagining.

When you go on a journey you often go via somewhere else to get to your destination. Then one day some of you discover a direct route which appeals to you more; it is easier, faster for you. That does not mean there is anything against the old route, it is just different.

Now you, my child, have not found it difficult to believe that Jesus speaks direct through Paul Tuttle, nor White Eagle direct through Grace Cooke, and latterly that I speak direct through Neale Donald Walsch. You did not approach these people or writings without thought, doubt, slight misgivings. After re-reading much of these writings plus previous ones including Annie Kirkwood and others, you became convinced that it was Truth with a capital T.

When you started this project you found it difficult to accept that you also were getting Truth. You doubted a lot and I kept saying to you Trust. Now you rarely doubt, but you find this contact too easy fully to comprehend. Why should you not be that "Channel for My Light"? You have been preparing for a long time, in your measure of time, to do this work. You have needed to keep your feet on the ground even if your head is often in the clouds! You are strong enough to withstand the criticism when it comes, as come it will. You already know that. But you also know it is worth the wrath of many, even if you help only the few.

Having read what I explained in Neale Donald Walsch's "Conversations with God" Book 3 about Revelations, you thought you would re-read the Bible account. You found it no easier to understand than previously, even though you had understood my further explanation through Neale. Now although all that I convey to you now seems easy to understand, to you, there will be many who read this and feel just at much 'at sea' as you felt yesterday with your Bible. Remember it is over forty years since you first began to seek in depth. Many who start reading these later writings will be where you were forty years ago – and they may not already be seekers.

You have a saying on occasions that 'there is all the time in the world'. Since there is no end to Life, it really matters not how long some souls take to remember where they came from originally. What is important is that there is not 'all the time in the world' to stop mutilating your planet. It is urgent that steps are taken now to stop this destruction, the thoughtless mismanagement of your resources. I shall keep saying STOP, think, change

34

your tactics. Your Earth and 'all that therein is' is surely too precious to be wantonly wasted.

You, my child, were told by one of your wise friends many years ago, all people would become vegetarian, then later no one would HAVE to work, and I tell you money will become non-existent. You will live by Love, true brotherly love, not only for each other, but for all creatures. You will require less sustenance, therefore the fruits and seeds will feed you. Your large animals exist on leaves, fruits, nuts, grass. Compare the size of their bodies with yours. You will not crave for rich food any more than most of you do now for drugs.

Oh, I hear some of you say, how boring life will be! No, my children, it will be wondrous and you will find new talents, with time to use them. You will be a sharing world. You will travel, but you will not try to conquer. To each his own. Does it not appeal to you to start the ball rolling for eventual Utopia?

Through Neale, I said how unevolved this planet is. You look at the busy lives of ants, bees, insects and think how boring that must be – with what end product? Well, that is how more evolved Beings look upon your planet. What is Your end product?

Think well on these things. Keep an open mind. Search for more understanding. Try to help those less fortunate, knowledgewise, than yourselves.

Give of yourselves to yourselves and the harvest will be brilliant.

PRAYING FOR OTHERS

1.12.00 Noon

Normally I would not be starting to 'tune-in' at this time because most days at noon I tune-in differently by praying instead of listening, by quieting my mind and putting myself under that wonderful Star of Light, the Christ Light, and mentally calling the names of all those on my list. These are the names of all those who need extra help, strength, comfort, healing. They are known to me personally. Then I add the Countries that are in trauma, at war, suffering from floods or drought.

Now YOU know all this dear God and you know how I go about this particular work which I have been doing for so many years. I feel I can explain, myself, what happens, but will you describe it for my readers please.

Jesus said, "I am with you always." He meant my Spirit is with you always, at all times. Many of you know this, some of you forget this and others of you are greatly comforted by this. I AM with you always. We are all One and cannot be separated.

When you are ill or distressed or depressed it is a comfort to you to know that another human being is caring enough to be praying for you, thinking of you. You find it easier to use another vehicle at that time, a sub-power station.

You leave a small light, or a reflected light, shining for your little ones when they go to bed; they find this comforting, either before they go to sleep or if they awake in what would have been darkness. A light is there. Some of those little ones have a tiny fear of the dark, others have a great fear of the dark. The light is comforting.

When you are 'on the rails' it is still comforting to most of you to know there is someone in front of you, or at your side, or behind you. When you have veered off the rails, even temporarily, it is even nicer to feel someone else is doing your sensible thinking for you. It is good to know you are being loved enough for someone else to care.

Now that 'someone else' is holding you spiritually in a wondrous Light, so powerful, so bright that it touches your very soul and helps you to feel better, even those of you who do not understand very much. You begin to wonder, to think, on a higher level. We cannot alter your choice, but we can raise your hopes, your feelings, your awareness to something better than you are experiencing at the moment.

You can 'wake up' to this Light, this awareness when you are ready. If you will remember that you are all one with each other, that no permanent harm can come to you, you start to feel better. You lose some of your fears. I keep saying there is nothing to fear. This Light is the Light of God, the essence of Good. I keep referring to the little ants – when the sun shines it doesn't pick out just one ant or a small group of ants, it shines on all of them. Sun, shelter, food is there for all of them, not just the tiny one. My Love, my nearness is there with all of you. I do not push some of you out as unworthy of my care. Remember that. You are all worthy of my care and it is always there for you.

I already know your needs and when your names are mentally called I already know each one of you, better than you know yourselves. I already know all about you. Liken this to your children, you already know where they are, where they are making for, how they are feeling, when they are frightened. I can only give you that inadequate analogy, because you cannot yet know the enormity of the Good that is around you at all times.

Think of a stage setting. A very large spotlight comes from above and lights the whole stage. All players are in it, can feel it, can see it. Then when one actor speaks, a strong spot light shines on that person or persons, because they are saying or acting something important. You are not completely out of the light, but for that moment it seems concentrated particularly on certain aspects of what is being portrayed. You can move into that extra light or it can move over to you and pick you out temporarily. But this does not mean that no light is there.

If the stage is plunged into complete darkness, those of you looking on know that this is only temporary and shortly the play, the story, will continue. It may show a completely different scene, but the players will be the same as those you have been watching earlier. Sometimes they have altered their costumes, or wakened up to a different life or attitude or outlook.

The darkness is only what you thought you saw and it was only temporary. You liked being in the light. In the light was all colour, movement,

(Here, I was interrupted by an important phone call. After returning to my computer some time later, note how the sentence was immediately finished off! I gasped in astonishment.)

warmth. You were not alone.

When you shake hands with someone you are acknowledging their presence, you are filling in the gap that you thought was between you both. You are acknowledging the presence of another. I tell you, there is never any gap. You are all One. Then you join together by holding hands in a dance or a celebration; you are giving out joy and love.

If you stand back, you are missing out on that feeling of well-being. If you stand back in resentment you are punishing yourself, but that little bit of resentment is too small to have any effect on the others. If you gather a lot of others around you and, because you have chosen those whom you think will feel as you do, you swell out that resentment and add more and more negativity to it, you temporarily cause a swelling that others can feel. You notice I call it a swelling. That is because a swelling is an absence of the space you thought was there. This swelling impinges on those who are rejoicing. Because there are more of them, it causes only a temporary disruption. As more join in the rejoicing the swelling gets busted. When it has gone, nobody misses it; it is as if it had never been there. But the rejoicing has remained, giving a state of happiness and wholeness.

See now how your holding temporarily dis-eased souls in the bright Light, you have strengthened them against negativity, against the false feeling of those who would be, or try to be, destructive in their influence. When you go out in the rain you put on a covering to keep you dry. However, should you get wet, you dry yourself out, but if you are feeling weak you need help with the drying out.

My children, try to be positive at all times, do not accept negativity. Choose, choose, choose always for yourself to experience the positive, the best for you at that time, and the best will come to you. Sometimes this comes in subtle ways, so subtle, that you are unconscious of it at the time. You can choose from little things like finding a parking space to reaching the moon. But do not choose for anything that will harm your fellow men, your brothers and sisters. Be grateful, be thankful, be happy and you will look in the glass and see yourself as I see you – happy and smiling and content.

Read and re-read all that nourishes your soul. You will find you alter your way of thinking about all situations and all people. Choose to be my child, my perfect child in whom I am well pleased. I love you all so much. Remember, remember, remember.

BREAKDOWN OF SOCIETY

I am getting more and more concerned by the increase in drug-taking, muggings, murders and road rage. We seem unable to cope with this quickly enough. Where are we going so wrong?

There are situations where humankind gets used to conditions. If you are in continuous pain, you get used to living with it. And as time goes on it doesn't seem so unbearable as it was. Your weather conditions are changing and you take the attitude – oh well, what can we do about it? There is more crime and violence and pornography on your television screens and you, the majority of you, think what can I do about it? You start to accept what is NOT the inevitable.

38

It is not natural to suffer great pain; it is not necessary to endure great weather changes; it is not acceptable to see such terrible suffering through the horrific treatment of the few to the many.

This is happening because the majority are leaving the cure to the minority. Not enough of you are saying, 'no more, we are not going to accept these conditions.' As I have told you before, thought is mighty and when enough of you stand firm against suffering of all kinds, there will be a shift. Your anti-vivisectionists have made a difference to your inhumane treatment of your brother animals and to such an extent that little mammals are even being given complicated surgery.

Re-read what I have said about giving love and discipline to children right from babyhood. [Page 29] There is nothing un-masculine in giving out more love to all humanity and all creatures. There is something missing when females become indifferent to the real needs of their offspring, when teachers are taught to be afraid of touching small children when they have hurt themselves. A new fear has crept in because those children are now taught to look for trouble, and try to use power to have that kind act misinterpreted. This is complex, but man has made it so.

The fastest way to improve all these conditions is to think more deeply, to return to being feeling, thoughtful, unselfish. When that wonderful time comes when there is no longer money, all will be so different.

Until that time, and to hurry it along, more and more of you need to put forth your good thoughts, your deep thoughts; to alter your teachings; to alter the way you bring up children. When television programmes shock and sicken your judgment, do not take it lying down. When enough of you start to say 'NO', notice has to be taken. The 'man who pays the piper calls the tune', remember that.

It is up to each one of you, of whatever age, of whatever education, of whatever position in society tomake your voices heard for the good of all. If you would have the courage to display no more violence, no more drug use, no more abuse on your screens, the immature minds would pick up a different perspective of what is a right and normal way of living and behaving. You encourage others to think all this violence is normal, the quarrelling inevitable, accidents commonplace. Reverse these thoughts. Expect good instead of evil, peace instead of war, health instead of disease, unselfishness instead of greed. It is up to you.

I have given you free choice – why do you choose the darkness instead of the light, the doom and gloom instead of the peace and beauty which surrounds you at all times. You have shut your minds and your eyes to a better way of life, for everyone. Guidance is awaiting you at all times from higher minds, higher beings, who look on in sorrow and amazement at your ignorance and acceptance of the unacceptable.

Be strong, be aware of your power for good. Be vigilant.

COMMUNICATION WITH GOD

I know that "You are closer than hands and feet; nearer than breathing" as is said in the White Eagle Lodge Healing Service. Please talk to me dear God. I have learned to distinguish between my thought and the thoughts, the words, that You put through me. It is such a subtle difference. To describe it to others is as difficult as describing a sunset to a blind person. How would you describe it, dear God?

I use only the words that are in your head, your personal dictionary. I could not communicate with you in Russian.

I heard Vi Parker, the medium, speak in North American Indian, when in trance. That was uncanny.

You are not in trance, my child. You are not being 'taken over' by another entity. You are listening to your higher mind. You are listening to your connection with, what you call, the Great Intelligence. Everyone can do this. You have referred to it as, in some cases, being your conscience. You can also use it as instinct. Animals use this knowing as instinct; flowers, vegetables, trees, have a wonderful instinct. It is natural to all that lives on your planet.

We have talked before about not being able to see Love, fear, jealousy, instinct itself, but you know they are there. It is easy for you to accept the first three, but you mistrust the fourth, instinct. You doubt it. Instinct is ME, it is Me making myself felt to you. There are those who doubt Love, fear, instinct; they brush it aside as imagination. There, you see, we are back to using imagination. Yes, of course, you can imagine silly things as you say, but perhaps it helps you to say there are two kinds of imagination. You can make up imagination with your mortal mind; you can write stories, you can invent stories, but you cannot invent Me.

What you, yourself, do is to become calm, still, then you listen and because you have emptied your everyday mind of all thought, I can speak to you in this way. And I know you love to listen.

40

You have been wondering what I feel on your Christ Mass day. As I am the All, I do not feel either happy or sad by your different re-actions to this festival. I see vast amounts of money being spent on food and gifts one for another and there is love in that giving and receiving. Then I feel the love and rejoicing deep in the hearts of those who really think about the Christmas Celebration. Thanksgiving and joy are expressed through prayers by remembering the birth of my beloved son, Jesus. Christians bless him for his time on earth, his birth, his Ascension, when he taught his followers about me and how to reach me. I was able to speak through him and he did not distort my Truth. It is those who have passed on his words where some distortion has arisen.

The teaching of Jesus was very simple, as are the words I tell you now. You all know, in your hearts, in your soul, what is right and what is wrong. I never asked Jesus to 'dress up' in order to speak to Me or to the people. Rise above material things, literally. You do not now put on a special gown to do this work. Would you feel any different if you did? Do you think I could speak through you more easily? No. I am speaking to your Mind, not your body. I am speaking to the medicine in the bottle, not the bottle. I am speaking to your soul, not your hat and coat. There is no space between your soul and Me.

For this reason, you, all of you, can help others by speaking to me about them. They do not have to be in your presence, or wearing certain clothes, but they are always in my presence. There is no space between Me, you and them. I am talking to all of you now who pray for others; those who do healing work. The work does not need loud words, loud proclamations, a great crowd present. Just know Truth in your hearts. Know that you are all my perfect children. There is no space. You are all equal. I do not judge. You have no need to judge. Because I know All, not one of you is 'on the outside', absent from my Love. Some of you are just not conscious of it.

If you are not in the presence of your children, your parents, your beloved, you know that they can still be with you at all times in thought. And this applies to those who have passed on. There is no separation on earth or between those on the earth plane and those on higher planes.

Very few of you know real, true happiness. You touch it some of the time, but not all the time. As you evolve you know joy, beyond your comprehension, at all times. When you rise above your suffering you are not made unhappy by those you love not experiencing your joy, for you know once they have come into this glorious state of at-one-ment they will be as whole and happy as you are. Look at it as they are having a bad

41

dream. You awake from a nightmare and are glad to find yourself out of that dream. The dreamers just need to wake up, either now or later, but wake up they will.

Go about your earth life in all the joy you can, giving off happiness and love. That is a great way of helping others. We use all the awakened souls, in different ways, to lighten the seeming burdens of those still in their own darkness. Wake up, my beloved children, wake up. You are already in Heaven for heaven is not a place but a state of mind and you can experience it on earth. Do you not say, when exceptionally happy, 'I am in seventh heaven'?

So my Christ Mass message to all of you is 'be in seventh heaven'. Bless you my beloved children.

LOVE

22.12.00

This will be my last opportunity to tune-in for a few days. Use me as you wish dear God.

You are picturing yourself standing with your arms outstretched, looking up into the rays from the Christ Star. Absorb that light, knowing that it is filling every particle of your body. You are now light as a feather and strong as a horse! You are all light, filled with my love, and you will be taking this light and love away with you. Use it for there will be those who can benefit by it.

Feel only love in your heart at all times. Do not judge anyone.

You know that all that you give out, all of you, comes back to you. When you give out love, kindness and understanding, that comes back to you. Those of you who give out distrust, jealousy, negativity, receive similar thoughts from others of like mind. Hate is a vicious feeling and if you could see your aura you would see it flashing red. It comes like a thunder storm, crashing all around you and those within your space. It gets you nowhere, except further away from your peace.

Oh, my children, if only you would learn to be peaceful and thankful for all you have. What you have may seem little, but do you not know those who are worse off than you? One rose given in love is worth far more than a dozen given from 'duty'.

Louise Hay ["You Can Heal Your Life", p.120] has asked you to pay your cheques, your bills, with love and gratitude for the services you have received; not with resentment nor anger. Acknowledge the service you have received, pay your cash or post your cheque with love. You will feel better for doing that. Stop to think about it when you do it. Yes, even your taxes, which most of you so dislike, even resent, for by paying those you are enabling others to have more, for all of you to benefit by the supply of the needs of all your roads, your refuse collection, the upkeep of your town or village. While money is being used, make it go around and what you give out with love comes back to you with love. I have told you, when you stop using money you will be far happier, far more satisfied, far more loving.

Try to remember to bless everything, from the time you arise in the morning to the time you go to sleep at night. You have lived another day. If it was very good you will remember it. If it seemed very bad, know you have come through it. Be honest with yourself and kind to yourself by realising you have come through. Smile in spite of all. You have never been alone. I am always with you. Lay your head against me and feel my love. Let me feel your love unconditionally.

Seek and you will find; choose for good to come to you. Choose for guidance. Choose for health. Then choose all these for your fellow beings. Throw a ball against a wall and it comes back to you. Throw a ball up into the air and it comes down to you. Bounce a ball on the earth and it returns to you. Think about this. Make that a ball of golden light and see how it makes you feel. Now think of yourself as a being of golden light and see how wonderful you feel. Practise this.

Endeavour to start your New Year, your New Century, with more thought, not only for others, but for yourself. You need to love yourself to enable you to love others. Love is so powerful, my children. My desire is for you to be happy, healthy, wealthy and wise! Not wealthy moneywise, although there need not be wrong in that, but wealthy in spirit, overflowing with kindness, gratitude, thankfulness, joy, peace, and above all LOVE.

I am with you always.

— 2001 —

PEOPLE

1.1.01

I have travelled some distance during the last ten days and, though I have met some lovely worthwhile people, I have looked on at herds of pushing, grumpy, rowdy people who seem to care about no one but themselves. They stuff themselves with mounds of food, they shout, loll about, swear. I suppose I am being judgmental, but I so wonder how we are going to get through to these people how much nicer the world would be if they thought more.

I despair of the masses and it makes me wonder what you think of them, dear God. I know you will say you love them; that we are all equal, but it seems so hard to accept all this unpleasantness with love. I suppose I do feel 'better' than some of them and I should not. Sometimes I want to shout out, "Be quiet, look at yourselves, listen to yourselves. Have you a sensible thought in your heads?"

Think of children in a playground. They are let out between lessons and they shriek and shout and run into each other. They are letting off steam, as you call it. Then they go back inside to learn. They settle down. Sometimes something happens in their lives that calms them down.

These are as untrained children. They do not aspire to any higher feelings. They get pleasure from behaving as they do, from getting drunk. Sometimes it takes great catastrophes to raise their thinking. I will take care of them, you concentrate on writing for those who are ready to listen and learn. You have found peace and love, you are finding you need less sleep, less food, less entertainment. You do not feel deprived. You seek those of like mind and you draw them to you. You have rapport with animals and flowers more than you do with many human beings. You are preparing for your next work on a higher plane, though you have no idea what it will be. Stay calm, satisfied with what you are doing. The cloak of souls around you is getting thicker. You do not like writing that in case it is not true, but I tell you it is true.

Remind yourself that many others around you on the earth plane are very full of fear. Be an example of what you believe. Yes, all this can be published with the rest in your book. There are others doing this who are just as doubtful at times as you. You will encourage them, just as Neale and others have encouraged *you*.

I would so like the opportunity of meeting Neale Donald Walsch and again meeting Paul Tuttle.

All things are possible with me, God; through me. Remember Choose, Choose for your wishes to come true. You are experiencing love, shall I say loveliness, from many people. You give out love and it is coming back to you pushed down and running over. Savour it, thrive on it, progress on it.

You are a little tired this day. You are finding it difficult to keep your mind on one side, as it were. Come to me again soon my child. Bless you.

MAKING THE WORLD A BETTER PLACE

Please, please take over dear God. Perhaps I need to ask more questions. What is the worst aspect of our planet at the present time?

There is mainly a lack of optimism at this time. There is a greyness, a lack of energy. Enthusiasm is lacking in many areas. Governments are changing all over Europe; you do not seem able to find good, strong leaders. There is a seeking for pleasure more than work, a seeking for an easy way out, so to speak.

Pride in work is lacking. Second-best is becoming acceptable – in work-effort, in end products, in services. Too many people want too much for too little. You all need to feel proud of your work, your efforts, your end products. When pride in work is lacking, end products are only ordinary at best.

The Western World, as you call it, has become too divided between rich and poor, caring and uncaring, thinking and thoughtless, more grabbing than giving, therefore less sense of achievement. You all need achievement in whatever job you do. We are back to pride in work, whether it be cleaning windows to a high degree or making furniture of excellence. All work has its merits, however lowly.

When I gave you free will I also gave you will power. Be strong in your endeavours whether they be for physical achievement or mental ability or advancement. You can do all these things for yourselves without harming others in the process. Your stamina can be great just as can be your will

45

power. Be strong in your endeavours, your ambitions. Be resolute in your endeavours to make your world a better place, not just for yourselves, but for all your brothers and sisters on all parts of your planet. Your help is needed; those of you who have the privilege of education could do so much more for your less fortunate ones.

When catastrophes happen you show your stamina and brotherly love. Surely you do not choose for catastrophes to bring out your best. Let your best operate at all times. Become aware, wake up to the needs of others; choose to be of help and you will become so much happier. Watch children and animals showing their happiness, their pleasure, in their achievements. Look back to your own achievements and re-feel your joy. You, yourself, are feeling what you describe as bleak. Why? What has been taken away from you?

Nothing has been taken away. All I can think of is that I miss sunshine and its warmth. Yes, I do feel bleak, flat. I dislike these winter months once Christmas is over. I know I should not feel this way. I would like to hibernate from January to April each year. I long to be working outside again, enjoying sunshine, seeing new growth. I will Choose to feel brighter.

Choose to use this time to do this work for the sake of those it will help. Choose to be bright and cheerful and you will be. Choose to be helped in all that you do and you know what? I keep telling you, all of you, I am always with you. Feel my presence. God bless you all my children.

WORLD PROBLEMS

Now I am here ready for another message from you. I am appalled by the disasters that are coming to light, and at such a rate. The 'airways' are getting so over-crowded there is likelihood of a terrible crash. The trains and railway lines are in disrepair, the roads are congested. Then we now not only have BSE, swine fever, scrapey and salmonella, but our fish are getting contaminated with pollutants. The salmon we hear are in a terrible state, diseased and not multiplying. There is an increase of disease, and old illnesses are returning like TB. The lesson is becoming so clear to those of us who know it is all wrong to have upset your earth. Our weather is different too. Is this a lesson that is being shown to us in severity so that more notice has to be taken?

46

The pink rosebud you see has started to open a little. You have noticed this when you 'tune-in'. There is an awakening taking place. There is disturbance over all the world. An effort is being made to rise up from the greyness. Your rose is using great energy now as you watch it, lifting itself away from the velvet. It is full of strength, life, love. The love is portrayed by its colour. One day this rose will be fully open, standing upright and giving off a wonderful fragrance. That will happen when my children have learned to treasure their surroundings and all the beauty that is there for them, free.

There is slow movement now, but it will increase and as more minds change their thoughts in unison with their planet, the flourish will start to manifest. There is much slush to wash away. The pollution is rife; it is covering all things in the air, on the earth and in the waters of the earth.

There are many workers on this side leading you, guiding you, impressing you to alter your ideas. There is an awakening taking place. The Good must rise above the seeming evil; fear of ridicule holds some of my children back, but this is where you who are more fully awake can help those of your brothers. Spread your thoughts like seed whenever you have an opportunity. Try to be an example, without fear. Spread the word of Goodness.

Be strong. Know the Truth and the Truth will start to free others as well as yourselves. You have to put into practice what you believe. So much of what has been put into practice is for gain, greed. It is done with the wrong motive. Become open to guidance, all of you. You already know in your hearts what is right. The road ahead is straight and beautiful. Choose to take that road, not the side tracks which you think may be quicker, but only take you through thorns and boulders, through darkness. That is not my way and you know it.

My children do not have to enter a church or mosque to do what is right. They already know what is right in their hearts. Your prayers and thoughts have such great power, as I have told you before. Use thought and prayer to move forward in peace and safety. Come off the path of destruction.

Try to live more simply, not wanting so much you do not need. Push out the clutter and live in the space of peace and light and beauty.

Look for the Good changes taking place. There is a great surge into gardening and it is bringing much pleasure; more and more of you are giving up meat. Many of you are also stopping eating birds and fish. Discipline yourselves and particularly your children over what is eaten. You do not need half of what you consume and this causes many bodily ailments. Try to be wiser my children. I want you to be 'happy, healthy, wealthy and wise'. Re-read what I have said about this earlier in our talks. You soon forget your lessons! [Page 20]

You, yourself, have been re-reading about those Aborigines ["Mutant Message Down Under"] and it is hard for you to believe that they could be so happy and content with so little: no fixed homes, no apparent food, no possessions. You could all be so much happier and healthier by having less and doing more for each other. Think deeply my children.

That is enough for today. Doing the right thing is both easy and difficult for you! But it is so worth the effort and I am with you all the way. Remember that.

LOVE MAKES THE WORLD GO ROUND

There seems an urgency for me to tune-in, even though I have only just come home. I am here God.

You experience so much love in your life. Was there ever a time when, however hard life seemed, there was not someone there to love you? This receiving and giving of love, pure, unselfish love, is your sustenance. It works both ways for you. You give out, you receive. You receive, you give out. This love feeds and sustains you. Remember that you cause others to feel as they make you feel – cared for and needed. It is the most important emotion in human life – even the animals show love to each other, especially the parent/child/baby animal care and love.

You have a song about love making the world go round. You all remember the loving, happy times much more easily than the 'bad' times. All Life needs a form of love. All life responds to loving care. All life responds to loving thought. The more you give out, the more you receive. You know this in so many ways.

Think of the most love you have ever felt, or feel, then multiply it thousands of times and you will begin to understand and feel my love for you, my children. Why do you come to me with your troubles and your thankfulness? It is because you know that I can feel your innermost, your depths, be they despair or great joy. You are learning and remembering at all times. You are never forgotten by Me, your spirit father. Think of a web of gold thread all around you, protecting you, impressing you, upholding you. You are as light as a feather, a golden feather of light. When you get depression or sorrow remember that. You are a feather of golden light in my care.

There is nothing stopping you from rising up into that light and nearness to me. We are one. I am with you at all times. I can 'blow' you into the best place for you to be, I can 'draw' you back to me. As I have said before, you cannot get away from me. In your innermost you all know this. Some of you put an iron casing round that feather and pretend no feather is there. You mistakenly think it will be easier that way – not to have deep feelings, not to think deeply, yet you know I am with you.

You fear, you mistrust, you worry. All that time could be spent so much more advantageously, for your own good and the good of others. Love is both gentle and strong, and it is ever beautiful. Facial expression changes when a human watches a great elephant, or a tiny mouse, with its young. You are touched by the sight of that love.

When you feel angry, irate, hurt, irritable, drop off those feelings like you would a heavy muddy cloak; drop it off, step aside, know nothing good has changed because you are always a child of mine, loved and understood. Encourage others to do this. As you grow in true knowledge you find these negative feelings trouble you less and less. Even your expression becomes serene, portraying your inner calm. Practise more often 'being still' and knowing that I AM GOD'. Practise feeling wrapped round by my love and guidance, and your earthly life will become so much easier.

Love all that is yours, but do not be possessive. There is no need to cling on to material things. There is no need to cling on to love, because the golden threads of love will cling on to you.

Know my love at all times, recognise that it is always there, right where you are, around you, in you, carrying you. When you truly know this you cannot judge others. You are all equal; some of you are more awake than others. The day will come when you are all awake!

THE POWER OF THOUGHT

When I re-read what you have been saying I am so comforted. I am so amazed at the simplicity of your wisdom. I am also so enthralled by your words. I know that I must pass on this work. I no longer have any doubts that the words are yours for I could not, under any circumstances, be so wise. I want to start testing out the effect of reading this out to others, yet I hold back. Is it fear of ridicule, of being thought nutty? Maybe it was at first. I now think that is not the case. I believe it is because, to me, it is all absolute Truth and I do not wish another to try to tarnish it. I wouldn't mind the ridicule, but I would mind ridicule of this, your work.

As I read the latest book I have acquired by Thom Hartmann "The Prophet's Way" I am finding so much in it of what you have been telling me. All my 'special' books are reiterating what I have been writing. All are stressing the power of prayer and right thinking.

My mortal mind is thinking how 'thick' people are, how hard to convince about this better way of living and thinking. I suppose that is judging them?

You are realising more than ever before the Power of Thought, especially in your present reading. Give others the opportunity of learning from this work. Do not hide this work; many are craving to learn more about how they can help your planet. Although you know millions of Neale's books have been printed, you do not meet those who yet know his work. Don't you think that proves there is a gap right where you are? There is a gap waiting to be filled with more of my Truth. Some people are as greedy for the Truth to help the planet as others are greedy for material things.

You, yourself, do not have to convince others of my Truth. It is up to them and to Me. The right people will be led to you just as you are led to the right books, to confirm what I have been telling you, what I will be telling you. You are a bit doubtful at this moment that it is not your mind writing. Well, I tell you, your mind is enlarging and the difference between you hearing me and hearing yourself is getting less defined.

God, I do not wish that to happen because I feel it is very necessary that I go on feeling that difference. I see the pink rose has opened even more today, but I want it to stay 'lying down' on the velvet. I am not ready for it to stand alone. That is it, isn't it? When it becomes upright I shall be more on my own.

You know you will never be alone. How many times have I to tell you that? Look at that rose another way. When it stands upright in your mental picture it will mean you have gained much more confidence. Trust me, trust me. I know what I am doing, I know what you are doing, I know what you are thinking. I will not push you ahead too quickly, but you are becoming a much quicker learner than you were a few months ago.

Now you are doubting again. I tell you, you are picking up my thoughts, my words, much quicker. Stop doubting. All these months have not been for nothing. Would it be better if you were a slower pupil? The rose is blooming; I will not let it fade, will you?

God, no. I don't want that to happen. I just feel I am not ready for it to have opened out so much. I am afraid of reading too much into this symbol.

Do you think I will let you misconstrue my messages now, just as you have become such a clear channel? Of course not. You give yourself these blips to make sure your own thoughts are not impinging on mine. I tell you, many, many of your thoughts now are mine, without you tuning-in.

You know that vegetarianism is coming far quicker than you dared hope. You know more compassion is being shown to animals, even tiny insects. This is happening by the power of thought, thought from thousands upon thousands of my children. Now know the thought of Peace is getting through. Know that the Power of Thought is getting through so that the use of chemicals and drugs are losing their little power. My people are tired of being 'drugged', 'poisoned', having their own better judgment overruled. My children already know what is right and what is wrong. When enough of them use that power, there will be a great surge for only that which is natural and does not violate their bodies and their earth, their weather and their climate. Right Thought is more powerful than any drug. You can help the people to think right, think strongly, for Good.

Your Prime Minister said recently, "Education, education, education." That is what you ALL need, especially the young people, the seniors of the future, for young minds are very impressionable. They will enjoy learning to be sympathetic with the environment and kinder to their bodies. They will become sickened with the state of their food, their world, their health, as it is today. They will want to surge forward into the New Age. We will talk about The New Age soon.

That is enough for today, my child.

How I look forward to these sessions. I wonder how many people in the British Isles are doing what I am doing? Can I ask you questions like this, God, or are they unimportant?

There are a number of people delving into the Truth. Each has his own way. None of my children is exactly the same; you all have different finger prints, do you not? You all look slightly different from each other, your walk, your stance, your voice, your art.

You have been wondering about colour. Colour can convey your moods; you choose your colour for the day. You pick up vibrations from colours when you are sensitive. Women particularly convey their moods, their vibrations, by colour. But the same shade does not necessarily mean the same mood or vibration to each one at a certain time. To each his own. Colour is important to you personally, especially as you become more sensitive. You have always liked working with colour, especially with flowers. You have, you find, an at-one-ment with flowers. Even fruits and vegetables draw themselves to you.

Are some people colour-unconscious?

Are some people God-unconscious, Spirit-unconscious, thoughtfulness unconscious, taste unconscious? As souls wake up they become more conscious on all levels. The planet starts to become more beautiful. Some are waking up through noise, loud noise; the vibrations of noise are low, disturbing, unpeaceful. With awakening, the soul requires more subtlety, more beauty, gentler tones. You read about pure White Light, in which are all colours. You are gradually ascending towards that pure Light and when you reach it you will find it is full of the most wondrous colours. In that Light is all Peace, all Love, all that is beautiful, glorious, perfection on the highest level. But that is a long way off in your idea of Time.

Do precious stones, crystals, metals, have any effect on us?

I have told you before, it depends how much of you, your vibration, your thought, you put into these things. It all depends how much you give out to that object. Hold a potato and put love into it and you will receive a feeling from it. Pour wrath into an emerald and you will receive a negative, even a harsh, feeling from it. Hate a person and you will not feel love from them; love that same person and you will experience a glow from them that you would not have believed was there.

This talk makes it even clearer how important it is that we give out Love to all the world; unconditional, non-judgmental Love. At what stage are we from the Golden Age of world peace?

It will not help you whether I say millions of years or only dozens of years. All is NOW. There are no neat little envelopes labelled This Tomorrow, That Next Year, Nothing Now. You are each in your own hell or heaven.

I cannot understand why there is so much starvation and catastrophe for so many of our brothers and sisters in places all over the world. How can they exist in such ghastliness? What goes on in their minds? How much are they suffering or are they beyond feeling?

Time, as you know it, stands still for them. They exist for each day. They are in what you might call limbo. You do not know what they are learning, remembering, feeling. Are they not using themselves as a great lesson in compassion for those with so much materialism? Do you not think they might be giving of themselves to bring out compassion, gentleness, a deeper feeling from those who look on?

My seemingly better off children have much more opportunity to experience these conditions because of your television screens. The impact is great and can hasten the coming of that Golden Age. More and more of you are being made compassionate, less selfish, more giving, by the sight of these suffering souls. They cause deeper thoughts and feelings and that is helping the coming of Peace.

Can you begin to see that great sacrifice is being made by the starving and homeless to encourage the rich to be more compassionate. The scales are so uneven. It is only through prayer and thought and compassion that justice will be seen to be done.

Those of my people with plenty do not want to suffer like that, yet they could do so much more to help the needy. As I have said earlier, the more you give the more you shall receive; the more you love the more you will be loved. Few know the absolute joy of your earth life. Too many think it comes through material things.

Children and young people will become the conduit. Especially so when their education changes. When you pray, pray for the young as well as for the needy. It will start a blending of the two extremes.

I feel we need to pray for a completely new television channel. One where no violence is shown, where much suffering is shown, where much teaching is given in a subtle way, so that viewers of all ages pick up a new wave of thought that can be sent out. I believe there are thousands of people who want to watch more worthwhile programmes. Oh, how I would like to be partly in charge of it. Then I would like to watch the faces of the children and young people who were drawn to watch it!

Someone, somewhere can start this! What is stopping them? Perhaps the same feeling that stops you from passing on my words to others. God bless you my children.

* * *

I think it is time I wrote about some of my present feelings and thoughts.

The messages I have been receiving have had a profound effect on me. I am much more aware of my thoughts at all times. I am conscious if I make a judgment about someone. I am more conscious of all around me and of being grateful.

Every morning and every evening I say "I am happy, healthy, wealthy and wise" and I think about each statement. If I am not particularly happy I ask myself why, then meditate on any problem and pass it over to God. I rejoice in my health, full of thankfulness that at my age I can feel so good and mostly full of energy. As for wealth, I have all I need for the day and think about my warmth, food, friends, home, amenities. If there are items to be paid for in the immediate future I know I will have enough money. I have learned this through the years, but can still occasionally feel anxious if a big item crops up. But, always there is enough when the time comes for payment. As to Wise, yes I like to think I am much wiser than I was and I also like to think that I am much more open to learning. I am grateful for my capacity to learn what is helpful for myself and for others.

I shall never cease to wonder at the gift I have been given to tune-in to God, and so easily too. It is when I read through what I have typed from Him that I know it is not my little self, for much of it is so profound, yet always so simple.

I long to impart this new-found knowledge to others. The few who have heard my work find it remarkable. All find it helpful, peaceful, comforting, enlightening, as I do. And they seem to accept that it is from God.

I am thrilled to have found new books to read that are 'spot on' for what I am doing. Often I read something and then it crops up in my next message. Now you could say that is because I have just read it, but how do you account for the equal number of times when I receive a message, then read it in another's writings, as if to confirm what I have typed?

It is certainly true that I need less sleep, less food and less entertainment than I used to, as was pointed out in one of the messages. I have not eaten red meat for years, but now I have to give up chicken and fish after some of the programmes I have watched on television. I am convinced we are all being guided to vegetarianism. I also notice how many people are avoiding pesticides and weed-killers.

I am alarmed at the shortage of birds around, even in the countryside where I live, and there are not many bees and less butterflies.

I am shocked at the amount of food that is bought in packets, ready-made, with nothing to do except warm it up. Cooking is an art form in my mind, a creative hobby as well as a necessity. Few young and middle-aged people now make cakes and pastry, pies, puddings. The number of overweight people in the West is alarming. I will ask more about this on one of my tune-ins. Think I have already written about this much earlier on.

I can see why I chose to return to live in Suffolk. I am surrounded by thoughtful, loving people who care about each other and for our welfare. I love the Peace that is here. I do not miss the beauty of the Isle of Arran like I thought I would, for although I adore mountains and woodland and marvellous views, I have such strong pictures of Arran in my mind that I can recall almost every mile of that island at any time I try.

One of the most difficult decisions of my life was to leave Arran. I was torn between my son and family, the beauty, the work we had gone to do, then deserting it. But I had such a strong feeling that I had to go. It hurt, greatly, but once here I knew I had made the right decision. I have no regrets, only joy in all that is now happening. I am convinced that nothing happens by Chance.

I treasure the love that is shown me by my family and friends, and acquaintances. It is sometimes as if all my senses have increased. I can find beauty in so much and pleasure in so little. My simple meals are sometimes a feast to me, attractive, tasting good, satisfying, wholesome.

Yes, I am progressing along my particular path and I hope God agrees. I must ask him!

* * *

CARE OF OUR PLANET

I long to be in touch with you again, God. When I am not, it is like being outside a door in the rain, when inside there is warmth and love awaiting me. I think of the grey velvet and that beautiful pink rose.

My love envelops you. You have just put yourself inside that rose and you can feel my love and warmth surrounding you.

You are witnessing much trouble on your planet and you do not like what you see. You have all been warned about the way you are treating your earth plane. Mainly you do not heed. Greed and selfishness, thoughtlessness and penury are rife.

You are witnessing disasters every day all over the world. You are draining the earth of her blood, the oil that has formed over millions of years, the trees that have developed over millions of years. You are polluting the water, both the seas and the rivers, you are destroying the structure of the land. You live for today, blow tomorrow.

Some of you are learning better ways and you feel like voices crying out in a desert, unheard. But you are not unheard. Every day more and more of my children are becoming more conscious of what is being done and are trying to make amends. Every one that starts being willing to make amends is adding strength to the others. You are too close to see the impact of these right thoughts. There are better ways to live your lives. You are ill from pollution, disease is spreading because you have misused your bodies and their immunity. You have made yourselves susceptible to what you call viruses and bacteria. These tiny microscopic organisms were always there, but you had resistance to them and they caused your bodies no harm.

On the one hand you have become over obsessed with cleanliness and on the other hand you ignore common-sense precautions.

Your minds can become dirty just as your bodies can. You need soap and water on your bodies and clean-thinking for your minds. Do not paint just the outside of your house, clear out the attics and cleanse the rooms. So much dust and fluff needs blowing from your minds and so much grease and poisons from the organs in your bodies. But you do not want to think on these lines.

I gave you free will, but I did not give you no will. I gave you strong will, not weak will. Apathy is, you think, an easy way out. You no longer like words like duty, conscience, moderation, thrift, unselfishness.

Your world has become a place of extremes, the very rich, the very poor, those with several homes and cars, those without a roof, those with food to waste and those who are starving. Now your weather is in extremes – too wet here, too dry there, too windy in one place, overheated and airless in another. There are those who will tell you it has always been so, but I tell you not in the way it is now.

Listen to those who are making new discoveries for fuel, power, transportation. And to those who are making better use of resources; to those who are 'discovering' the improvement in health by different eating habits; more, but less strenuous exercise. The pendulum has swung too much to the left of centre. Centralise it by becoming willing to listen and learn.

I shall keep saying pray, pray, pray. Ask for a better world, see it coming, see Good happening and, you know what, you will see an improvement. The more of you who take heed of what I am telling you, the sooner you will see improvements.

Use your voices, your words; demand to be heard, but not by force. I do not command you to do anything, because you have free will, but for my sake use your free will for Good. Become channels for light and guidance. You cannot command me nor I you, but you can demand each other for a better, more equal existence. You are still so afraid of being a loser. Your shares may go down, but your share will go up and those who have never had shares or a share, will become rich.

Trust, Love, Pray, Believe, have Faith, have Compassion. These are the attributes that will bring you the World, the New Age, that you all long for in your hearts.

Do more homework, not in your houses, but in your minds. I have spoken very seriously to you today. I suggest you heed my communication.

The poor and starving want to be rich, but the rich are afraid of being poor, they do not truly want to share. Are you happy to be so unequal? Give, give, give instead of take, take, take. You will be HAPPIER in so doing. Trust me, believe me. I love you but you do not like being admonished. Remember I know each one of you intimately, nothing is hidden from me because we are all part of the Great Intelligence you call God.

Bless you my little, little children. May you Wake Up.

HELPING THE WORLD

I enjoy receiving all this, dear God, but it is doing little until it is printed in book form. I type, then I read and absorb what you have said, but what can others do, even when they have read this, and works by Neale, Paul Tuttle and others? How can the 'ordinary man in the street' help. I know you will say Pray. Yes, we can all pray for a better world with a fairer distribution of goods, but what else can we do, practically?

Little groups of like-minded people can form. You remember what Jesus said 'When two or more are gathered together in my name.....'. Try to involve all ages, including quite young children. Discuss local issues you would like changed. If in a town, discuss what people you could contact who could carry your thoughts forward; your councillors, Members of Parliament, Police Officers, teachers, environmental officers. If in the country; your farmers particularly, your parish councillors, your clergy, your doctors, vets, nurses – all those who come into contact with others and use forms of the environment. You know yourselves how you want conditions to alter. Choose spokespeople who are calm and confident in their subjects and who can suggest improvements.

There will be a snowball effect when enough groups gather and voice their right thoughts, both in public and in silent prayer. When groups get too large to gather in private houses, book inexpensive venues and ask for donations afterwards. Then trust, TRUST, and enough money will be collected to meet expenses. Give of your time, hold discussions, always remembering to be sincere and calm. Heated arguments will only destroy what you are trying to build up.

It is up to the 'public' to have what they wish implanted in their children's minds as well as planted in their fields.

Know, know, that when you do right, think right, act right, there will be an improvement. From small acorns great oak trees grow. Remember the story of the loaves and fishes. Amongst you you will be able to collect clothes, equipment and food to send abroad and there will be those who are so big hearted they will give of their wealth to pay for transporting the goods.

This is a beginning and it will grow. Believe me, it will grow. All these acts will be done in Love and that Love will go forth in great waves of strength. I will send you leaders, people who will guide you when you feel inadequate. Trust me, as I so often ask you to do.

Keep the Light shining over yourselves and over your work at all times. The Light will protect you and all that you do, especially when some of you choose to go abroad. That Light is Love and Strength and Protection. Try it over those you love, put it into daily use within your family, use it over your friends when they are in trouble or ill. Test it for yourselves. You can ask this writer about this. She has used it for years and has found its strength and comfort.

So this is how you can help your world. It is a beginning and it will be blessed a hundredfold.

Bless you my children.

ON THE EDGE

A thousand thoughts have just been rushing through my mind. The book I am reading is making me so aware of the homeless and starving. Then I look at our shops, even in our small market town, bulging with clothes and food and housewares.

I have also been reading about 'being on the edge' and I found it difficult to grasp, but now I think I understand. We can be on the edge of our land of plenty and endeavour to enter the edge of the lands of poverty. By discussion and endeavour could we form Help Groups, then choose an area of extreme need, say 'on the edge' of Russia? Would we get permission to 'adopt' this area, then collect goods and a means of transport to start up what I should like to call A Circle of Light. Could we become a starting point of many of these circles, perhaps joining them together, not at their source, but at their point of help, so that a tiny group abroad could become an area?

However little income we have, we could purchase a few suitable items each week; we could ask shops if they would join in. We could ask for surplus from charity shops. We could find out if we could have diesel without tax. The only money we would need would be for transport. We could stick just to our own group. I am against going through any charitable organisations for I have learned how much money is wasted 'training' people, buying equipment, red tape, etc. Am I being naive or is this a way to begin? I know we would require an interpreter and a driver and permissions of entry.

Please tell me if this is a beginning, or am I just wasting my thoughts?

You know that all these things are possible and you know similar ideas have failed in the past. Success will depend on dedication, unselfishness and prayer.

You do not realise the enormity of what is required. You could learn from others who do this work. The Red Cross would be able to give you advice. Great dedication is required. Give this more thought. You know that thought can become reality. You know that no good thoughts are wasted. You know that I am here to guide all my children.

Is this an inspiration I have received, dear God, or just wishful thinking on my part?

All right thought, all inspiration, all ideas, come from the Great Intelligence. Remember what I have been telling you. Push out doubts, negativity. Think positively and with maturity in all things. Appeal to others to help your world. Ask for their ideas. Remember about little acorns.

Bless you, my child and all my children.

DEATH

May I ask you, dear God, why my old friend is 'hanging on' so long?

You can see your pink rose as a bud again and lying down. It is peaceful, but you can see it looks asleep. It is taking a rest. It doesn't want to wake up just at this moment in time. You notice I call it a moment. That is all it is, an earthly moment.

When the 'time' is right it will awake and it will find itself in its new wondrous surroundings. Be patient. That soul is in our care and we are ready to receive her back from where she has come. Do not disturb that last peace. She is not suffering, only the mortal mind is clinging on, just temporarily.

You, none of you, have to carry any blame for the life of another. You all have free choice. You cannot take over my work. Wrap Love around those you care so much for, and wrap love around yourselves.

You are right to remember, "Let Go, Let God." You can best help by knowing there is no separation, yet each is its own personality.

Read her daughter what you have written. She must learn to love herself and to know that she has done all possible for her beloved mother. She has done a great deal more than many do for their loved ones. I can see into the hearts of all of you. Nothing is secret from me. I understand. I love you all. I know when you are trying your hardest to do and think what is right. Now leave the rest to me.

God bless you ALL my children.

HOW TO IMPROVE HOME CONDITIONS

Every act of kindness you, my children, do, goes out in waves and multiplies. This is why prayer, true prayer, unselfish prayer, benefits others more than you can realise.

I keep telling you, much prayer is needed for all your planet. Do not accept that you cannot improve situations, however enormous they seem to you. We look on from our higher plane just as you look on at the little ants on a small piece of ground. You can see their mingling. Sometimes you see their purpose, their organisation. They are running hither and thither and instinct guides them. They use this instinct; they know it works. My children mainly do not follow their instinct, their conscience.

I have talked about this before. [Page xx] Do not think you are helpless to improve world conditions. Prayer is so powerful and can cause action to be taken. The few CAN help the many. SEE a better world, improved conditions, an improvement in the treatment of your earth plane.

Choose to be of use; choose to be guided; choose to be used to help others. Do you not think it is significant that TV programmes are 'choosing' to portray the experiences of living in past times. There are those who are choosing to experience what it was like without having so much. Participants feel how over-worked their forebears were, spending long hours doing work that is now done by machinery.

The children are not finding it as difficult as their parents. The children are finding they can be happy making their own amusement, using their ingenuity, playing with each other. It is the adults who are saying they are so tired with the work, yet their ancestors were only healthily tired, bodily tired. Now in the present time they are tired mentally. Manual work is now made easier, but they are stressed with mental work and worries about finance because they are not satisfied to live within bounds applicable to their incomes.

Do you think people were less happy then than 'now'? I tell you, all is now; you have lost the art of living together, of striving together as families. There is so much unnecessary dissatisfaction.

Recall how those people felt, having lived on the Isle of Taransay for a year. They knew freedom from cares; the harshness of their conditions did not harm them. Mostly, you heard them say, they wondered how they would re-join life as they had known it. You have lost the freedom I have given you. You are governed mainly by the greed of others, by 'wants' you really do not need.

Take heart from the small improvements that are being made; from compassion that is being shown to all forms of life. What do 'bullies', 'winners' and 'dictators' really gain for humankind as a whole?

Follow what you know to be right, to be kind, to be for everyone's benefit. Good is effective, it is stronger than you can see. It is sometimes too near for you to grasp, but it is within your grasp. Look forward to a better world, help it to happen by your right thoughts, by your dedication to good. It is so important that you train your young ones' minds in the right way of living, thinking and behaving. Every word, every action of the older affects the younger.

So many of your worries and troubles are caused by your feelings of not having enough money. You spend what you have not got; you want what you do not need. Look more deeply into the lives of those around you. Those with little, are they not often happier and more contented than those of you always wanting more?

Life in all its other forms knows nothing of money, of paying for all its needs, yet how many of my birds, animals, insects, go short of food and shelter, except where man has deprived them of it? Read about the lives of tribes, isolated tribes, who live by their instincts. When left to their own resources they do better than where so called civilised man has interfered with them.

Try to learn my children. You have so much to learn, to understand, to remember. Give more of your time, your thought, your goods, to others and expect nothing in return. I, Good, will repay you. Treasure, succour, love your earth. Treat it kindly. Look at all nature as a lesson to be learned by you, my little, struggling, infirm children.

MAKING A DIFFERENCE

7.2.01

Are we still heading towards disaster or has the new Golden Age started?

Look for the signs of a better future. You need to look hard. You are encouraged by what you have heard children being taught and talking about. After a really bad storm there is a lot of clearing up to do.

You have noticed signs of new life appearing in your garden. Those shoots and bulbs use great strength to make an appearance; they seem slow to you to move into visibility. Today you saw yellow crocus actually in bloom; just a few, tucked away where you had not previously seen them. What colour? Bright gold. Yes, there is movement towards a better way of life; it is slow, not everyone is interested.

You are still like voices crying out in the wilderness; more of you have to shout louder for a better world.

Do our scientists and archaeologists need to spend so much time digging about for knowledge of the past, and counting chromosomes, testing DNA? Pumping sick people full of drugs and chemicals, often doing seemingly more harm than good?

You can learn from the past, you can remember from the past. As for the present, damage is being done. You already know how chemicals have affected the soil and the plants. Often you can see how drugs and chemicals are adversely affecting the human race. You can Choose to work differently. You can Choose not to mutilate your bodies and your earth.

What do you think about testing being done on animals?

I have told you many times, in many books, to treat your animals only with love. Animals are mute; they cannot complain to you about their treatment. Humans can decide for themselves whether they wish to be used as experiments. Humans can decide to go flying, to climb, to swim, to take risks. If you are not willing to take risks, tests, why should your brother animals be made to do this? Who is there to 'stand up for them'? Why, humans, and a few do. As I have said before, when enough of you make yourselves heard your commands will be heard. You let your army, navy and air force chiefs command you to do their will, whether you like it or not. Why do you obey them? Because you still think you need your armies. You fear for your safety, your lands, your lives.

Only know that you are already taken care of. You do not need armies, fighter planes, bombs, guns, weapons of destruction. You have not learned, in all this time, to be peaceful, to be calm, to be trusting. What example are you being, all of you? You kill, you mutilate, you poison, you frighten, you terrify each other, nation to nation. How can you consider yourselves civilised? If you were given a questionnaire, how many of you, in all countries, would choose to tick that you wanted to live in this continual fear of each other? If you were really honest, would any of you choose to live as you are? You come into the world with nothing, materially, and you leave with nothing, yet you live your lifetimes mainly fed and watered, housed and looked after. And you are living longer in earth years than in recent centuries.

Now I am not including the starving in some countries, where there are thousands of them. You know about them. And what do you do about it? I told you earlier on, they have chosen, by great strength of character and love, to come here to be an example in the hope of bringing out your compassion. How well are they doing?

You care for pet animals, sometimes to excess, yet you torture and destroy large creatures as if they had no feelings. You care, sometimes in excess, for your own children, yet you ignore my children in poor countries. What do they have to live for? What treats do they have? What hopes? Could you not find great happiness in helping the starving to live a better life, to pass on your skills, to learn about their needs, their resources? Why do you think you need so much? Do you think you impress others more with your cars and your jewels and your designer clothes than you would by displaying your courage and endeavour in helping those without even a shirt or shoes?

How do you think you are doing with your free choice? I am not judging you, I am asking you to judge yourselves. Would you be a proud parent if you let your children starve and go barefoot while you were luxuriating in everything that your money can buy?

Wisdom is free, love is free, compassion is free, thoughtfulness is free. These things are free to give and they need never run out. Would you not like to try using these free gifts more?

RISING ABOVE THE GLOOM

I was feeling a bit useless today, not getting anywhere, and not knowing what move to make next. Then I get a phone call that lets me know I am still of help to others. That is good to know and I am grateful. I am here to be used, to be occupied, for in spite of my age I cannot laze about. I could do with some good laughs just now, but they are in store I am confident. February is a gloomy month and the flooding is going on for so long. This, added to the trauma of watching a very sick friend, for so many weeks, just hanging on to life by a seeming thread, is pulling me down and I know that is wrong. Come through to me, dear God and give me some of your words to pass on.

Do you remember flying above the clouds for the first time, in brilliant sunshine, when you had left a grey, wet day below? That made you realise the sunshine is always there even when you cannot see it. Apply that to your life at this moment, for it is only a moment of eternity, and know you can rise into that sunshine at all times.

Recall past grey times in your life and notice how, now, they have become short episodes instead of long patches. They seemed so long when you were experiencing them – now they are as nothing because you have experienced such happiness in between. You cannot appreciate the sun without the shade, the heat without the cold, the joy without the sorrow. Come, my child, you can overcome your difficulties, always, especially now you are so conscious of my love always with you. You are never alone and you know that. You are never unloved and you know that. All your needs are met and you know that. Now remember your daily affirmation that you are 'happy, healthy, wealthy and wise'.

Remember I told you we do not waste our resources.

When you say 'we' how does it apply to you, God, He, She, It?

In this instance, WE means all those souls who are watching over you, helping you, guiding, all of you, in the best way to go. Call them my delegates if you wish. You will become one of them at another stage of your being. You are often nudged to remember to do something and you know it is not your own mind nudging you, and you say a quiet 'thank you'. Sometimes you, all of you, get more than a nudge, it is an inspiration or an enlightenment and it makes you feel very good. That is when you experience an at-one-ment with higher beings.

Choose, choose, choose at all times, whether it be for small or large happenings: the result, the action, then the thought, not the other way round. You have been learning this and finding it difficult to grasp. You have put it into practice with your daily affirmation and finding that is the order in which it is happening. Use this way for the bigger things you are considering. See the end, then the making of it happening, then the thought. Make the reality happen before the 'work' and lastly the idea.

THE RIGHT TIME TO DIE

I have learned that we are born at a specific time and that we die at a specific time. If this is so, why do we pray for the life of another, for them to get better, for them not to die? Or perhaps for them to die and not go on suffering? I know we should wish at all times 'for thy Will to be done'. This becomes a paradox.

It is taking you a long time to hear me because you have a fear of not hearing me properly on this occasion. You feel this is such an important question.

You are remembering what Raj told you when you asked him (through Paul Tuttle) about the difference between euthanasia, keeping people alive by mechanical means, or just letting nature take its course. He said it made no difference because that person would die when the moment was right.

When you talk to me about specific people, you are making a channel of Light, over yourself and over that person and others involved with them. By doing this you are making it easier for all involved to feel what is right, to feel what will be helpful, not only for the person who is ill, but for their loved ones. If you walk out into the night you are helped by using a torch; if you walk along a well-lit road it is easy to see where you are going; it is

66

easier to look ahead; you can even recognise others you know in that brightness.

Remember Time is not as you know it. Yes, there is a right moment for the soul to leave the earthly body, but it is not Time as you know it. Suppose someone is dying just as you alter your clocks from Summer Time to Winter Time, what would you say was their time of death if they passed at that moment?

Prayer, true unselfish prayer, is always heard and by putting yourselves In the Light, in the Channel, you are making it easier for all to bear those difficult moments between what you think is Life and Death.

Prayer creates Harmony, Peace. When you go from one room to another you pass at varying speeds and were you to fall between the two, you would get up, or someone would pick you up, and put you into either one room or the other. You would soon forget how long it took, but you would know which room you were in. If wise ones were helping you to get up they would know which room it was better for you to be carried into. This is assuming that you are, at that time, pretty helpless. The Guardian Angels of each one of you would be working for your best situation at that moment. Liken this to death. You are never alone, any of you, as I am always telling you. Some of you are 'awake' and others are not, they are not aware of Guidance.

You would be surprised at the thoughts of those around the sick and helpless. Those thoughts are not hidden from us. It is often good that you cannot read those thoughts for you would be surprised by either their selflessness or their selfishness.

Talk to me at these times, know that help is there for all of you and Love and Comfort will come to you so long as you are open to receive it. Strength also is being 'rayed' to you. This is often when you are nearest to me in the context of your mortal thinking. Ceremonies of all kinds can make you feel near to Good. Think about that.

Does that answer your question?

Yes, I think so for the time being. I need to think about it more. I hope I have been a properly clear channel, for this is such an important question.

LIVING IN ISOLATION

I know that you know, dear God, what is going on in my mind at all times. Do I waste a lot of my time in day-dreaming?

Let me say that you use a lot of your time in trying to sort out what you are learning, remembering. Mostly your thoughts bring you great comfort. Sometimes you have wondered what it would be like if you could live in an isolated Scottish croft on a hill, gathering your own fuel, being entirely dependent on yourself. You would like to experience being entirely self-sufficient, fighting the elements, overcoming the bitter cold. Why do you query that in your heart?

I think I want to overcome fears of discomfort, prove to myself that I am always cared for, never alone; know an environment where nothing could distract my meditations. Yet in my heart I know I couldn't endure extreme cold. Summertime, yes, I would like the experience. At my age I know it is a silly contemplation. I cannot say 'desire' for it is not strong enough for that, just a dreaming.

You are able to experience this isolation just where you are now. You are able to shut your door, cut yourself off and think your thoughts. Here you are doing it in the comfort you need. You can walk alone with your thoughts in the countryside, you can please yourself how you spend your days, you can eat little, cook little. You need warmth to function; your loving nature needs occasional company. Would it help anyone else if you cut yourself off, so to speak, for six months?

It was just a thought.

Not one of your more useful ones! Be patient, carry on the way you are. Be a good listener and a good learner. You know you have all you need at this moment and you are ceasing to 'want', knowing that it is OK to live for the day only. Do you not know that it helps others to know you are there? Enjoy your peace, your aloneness without being isolated; you appreciate the help and concern of those around you.

You want to reach the diamond in that rose, to find out what it means. You will. Do not be afraid of the stem becoming upright; I will not give you more to do than you can cope with. You know that. You have always experienced something truly to love in your lifetime – your Mother, your babies, your beloved husband, Stanley, your idyllic holidays caravanning in the Welsh mountains, the contact you have now with your grown sons.

All those things have been free for you, the cost has been negligible. You can truly say, each day, 'I am happy, healthy, wealthy and wise' – with my help you have made it so for yourself.

Go your present way in Peace. Continue to do my work. Continue to learn. Continue to Love all and bless all. I bless you my child.

GOOD VIBES – BAD VIBES

There are two questions I should like to ask today, please. The first is about vibrations, currently called vibes. Is this another word for atmosphere? People, houses, buildings sometimes seem to give off good or bad vibes. Can you explain?

You can create a sound, but you cannot see it. You can create a thought, but no one else can hear it. You can create a movement, but you cannot taste it. You can create an atmosphere, but you cannot see it. Where do you think those creations go? Nothing you create truly disappears. The thoughts, the sounds, the smells, go forth as vibrations in the atmosphere.

Nothing is lost, all is contained in The Whole. There is no space, remember? Water comes from clouds as rain; the water is drawn back as clouds. The noise from a jet engine at source is terrific, then it dissipates into the atmosphere. It has disturbed the air currents. All is movement. Vibrations are never still. You hear the noises, you smell the scent of flowers, or people, you recall noises, smells, tastes, tones, in your mind.

You pick up the quiet, the peace, in a church where much prayer has taken place. You do not experience that feeling in a disco hall. People who are what you call Sensitives more easily pick up the Vibes. They can feel danger, horror, ill-feeling. The more sensitive any of you become the more easily you pick up the vibrations.

So the answer to your question is, yes, vibrations can be picked up, for remember there is no time or space. Whether a murder was committed last century or last week there can be terror in the atmosphere. Does this help you?

I need to think deeply about this answer. My other query is, can we hold souls back, keep them earthbound, by clinging on to them mentally after they have passed on?

Say you have a small child; you are happy to answer all its questions, to be near it, to help it. As it grows up you expect it to fend for itself more and that gives you an opportunity to 'lead your own life' so to speak.

Now there is a difference between writing to a dear one every day or telephoning them every day instead of writing or speaking to them occasionally. The first can be rather unnecessary, the second method can be delightful and give great pleasure to both parties. You are not then interrupting or interfering with each other's different lives. It does not mean there is less love or more forgetfulness, just a different communication.

Your dog will come when you call it, but if it is busy chasing a rabbit it will be torn between duty and pursuit, love and fun, or rather obedience and instinct. It will love you anyway, but wants that bit of freedom to follow its natural instincts. Conversely, if the call is coming from the one who is on a higher plane, it may be to give you a warning or guide you in a difficult situation. You all have what you call common sense – use it!

Thank you, I can understand that answer perfectly.

BEING CLOSE TO LOVED ONES

Has my mother been close to me more often in the last few months; if so why? It has felt like that to me.

Your mother has always been as near as you wish her to be; there is a great bond between you. She is interested in all that you do and she is just as concerned about you as she always was on the earth plane, but she now knows there is no need to worry about you. On this higher plane there is no need to worry. We know that you are safe at all times and that whatever you do it is because you choose to do it.

I would say that it is YOU choosing to be near her. You look forward so much to being with her again. You realise that, in earth time, you are nearer the time of being with her again than you were forty years ago. Your dreams are sometimes becoming very real to you; the contact is very vivid. Rejoice in that.

Does Stanley know how often I think of him and send my great love to him? I feel he is very occupied with things beyond my ken.

There is no separation in true love. You have truly loved several people and animals during your earth life. Remember there is no separation in reality; there is only separation when you choose to make it so.

Stanley works on several levels – with the earth plane and on other planes, other planets. He is an advanced soul. You will again learn so much from him when you rejoin, just as you learned so much from him during your earth span together. You have been together many times and you both felt that. He is near you when you, so to speak, call him. But he knows you are always looked after and have many souls around you both here and on the earth plane, who are concerned for your well-being. You are learning more than you realise, day by day. You assimilate knowledge much quicker than you used to do. You are learning to trust your intuition and you no longer care whether others believe what you say or not! You are now sure of yourself. You have doubts some days, yes, but only temporary ones, you are soon back on this higher level of thought. You listen for guidance, you recognise guidance when it comes, you are letting go of many old fears and doubts. They did you no good and you are shedding them.

Please send me more people who are on my wave-length so that I can have meaningful talks with others.

Choose, choose, choose all the time. Live in each moment. The glories ahead will come to you at the right times, both on the earth and in this afterlife as you call it. You know there is so much to look forward to, but you are quite content to wait for everything to happen at the right time. You are absorbing understanding of there being no space and you are now beginning to absorb the fact of no time, but that is taking you longer. Be happy, be content. You are never alone. We never forget you, not even for one instant dear child. God bless you.

WORLD DISASTERS
22.2.01

Every day we see more and more disasters on our television screens. Foot and Mouth disease is back, apparently after a gap of twenty years. Now there are floods again in Africa. Last night I watched the terrible conditions in Rwanda. Where will it end? What are we doing about it? How many people realise the seriousness of all this? Farmers are

71

frightened of losing their livelihoods. Can't they see it would be better to give up livestock and not only go organic, but start to grow vegetables and nuts and grains for vegetarianism? This idea is cropping up in all these kinds of writings, but how many are heeding?

You are causing your own destruction in so many ways. You are learning the hard way. You do not heed warning signs. Thousands are being wiped off the earth plane by floods, disease, droughts, wars. Fear and anxiety are rife, blotting out the better means of survival. Man still thinks he knows best, knows his own remedies. Only great disasters are causing him more thought. Millions are learning how to live without money – admittedly in a seemingly dreadful state of poverty. But all this is the beginning of the Great Change that is to come.

Why is there this terrible disregard for common sense in connection with smoking and drinking. What is happening to our young people?

They think discipline is old-fashioned, out-dated. They do not heed their consciences – that too is old-fashioned. Their priorities are in reverse. Each for themselves; they care not for others. In one of your children's stories you referred to being "bird-brained". I tell you, the birds have much more sense of what is right. The few are going to suffer because of the many – the many who do not care. I have told you, and other writers, there is this lack of discipline right from babyhood. You are looking on and seeing what happens when undisciplined children go their own ways, for they are very little children. They are dis-using their brains and mis-using their bodies. You can tell if you either starve or overfeed your pets, then you usually rectify it for their own good and because you love them. What are parents doing for their young? What kind of example are they being? Do they think their neglect is love? I tell you, they do not know the meaning of love when they ignore the welfare of their children.

Those of you with more use of your intelligence can make your voices heard, but you seem loathe to do it. Is that not being an accessory after the fact?

My people have become so discontented, always wanting more and different experiences, not because of knowledge but because of greed. You are not satisfied to live in your own space; you are not interested in improving your surroundings, nor appreciating your surroundings even when they are commendable. You have forgotten the joy in small things; the joy of time together, the joy of giving and receiving in a small way, without vast amounts of money being spent. There is room for all of you on your planet; there is food aplenty for all of you on your planet; there is joy for all of my children, but they have forgotten how to find joy – in loving and giving, seeing and doing for others.

Each needs to have an opportunity of doing what appeals to him or her. Not every subject needs so many other subjects to make it 'learnable'. If art is a choice, it does not need maths and science; if science is applicable it does not necessarily need languages and art. There is a place for history and geography, but too much is being expected of many of your young. It is more important to learn about ancient herbs, cures, cultures than how to make bombs and tanks for destruction. All these things I have told you about in many places.

Do we need to be so busy with our own survival that we haven't time to think about conquering or interfering with others? Is that the way we shall have to go to improve our behaviour? Would that be a way of living in our own space?

Some of my children will have to experience great trials, sorrows and diseases to enable them to make sure their brothers do not have to suffer the same in the future. There will be those who choose to suffer, just as I told you the starving and homeless have chosen their existence to bring out the compassion in others. What more could be asked of man than to suffer for the sake of the whole, for the sake of the planet and those beings who are yet to come?

You need to become as little children to enable you to do my work, to feel my guidance, to feel my love. Enter your children's minds and see what you are doing through their eyes. No wonder they grow up with fears and feelings of hopelessness. Look through their minds and learn how to teach them what is right and loving. Give them a better picture of their future to look forward to. A child does not need much encouragement to learn to love and trust. Do not abuse that love and trust for it is a fragile and beautiful attribute. Think deeply my children.

LEADERSHIP & INTEGRITY

I know that we choose to come back, to re-incarnate in certain circumstances, to enable us to function in that position. Do we know whether we are going to make a success of the job or not before we leave the higher planes, the heaven world? I ask this because we look on and see the awful mess that leaders seem to be making of their jobs. They are often corrupt, devious, greedy, liars, unreliable – few seem to be good examples to the rest of the world. I am thinking of Presidents, Statesmen, Ministers in Governments, even lawyers and clergy, teachers and doctors, some of the police.

The love of power is heady stuff, whether it be in a small way, as teachers and priests, or in bigger ways as Heads of State, powerful Ministers.

The appeal of power, self-gratification, power over thousands of others, is so great that it sometimes outweighs feelings of Right and Wrong. Remember, too, that others, also with power, be it lesser power, encourage leaders in their search for yet more power. Even in little local councils there is often one man or woman who wants to be top dog, to sway others. In what you call high places the power becomes much greater, the ego puffs up, the feeling of importance beckons. Remember, others encourage this struggle to get on top, to be powerful.

It is a case of the few trying to sway the many.

We seem to have little choice in choosing our leaders when none appear to stand out as potential great, honest, people. We need more 'good' people to choose from. The good people are usually quiet, not seeking power and attention. What choice do we have?

Do you think you should look for more women to place in positions of leadership?

Look what happened when Margaret Thatcher was put into power – to start with she was good, then power went to her head and caused her downfall. I am not very hopeful of getting a good answer today!

You think I cannot guide you? You think there is no solution?

I don't know. I just don't know. We badly need better leadership, more honesty, more Truth, more true compassion. More done to make us more equal; not so much of the rich and the poor.

As yet it is taking a long time for those with compassion and care to make themselves heard and listened to. The 'bullies' seem to be winning; the know-alls are being listened to. Just as it is taking much time to get people to give up eating flesh, smoking, drugs, alcohol, so it is taking a long time to get them to see how much better off they are choosing,

CHOOSING, to alter. It is two thousand years since Jesus showed you a better way of living. How far do you think you have progressed?

That is very depressing help. I wish you would make us alter; it would be better if we did not have free choice, surely? Yes, I know we have to experience the bad to appreciate the good. But we are mainly so tired of waiting for a better world, a fairer world, a cleaner world. We so need your help.

I am here, at all times. Most of you do not heed me, do not use me. I will not take away your free choice or you will never learn. You are here to learn, to remember. Each one of you needs to be a good example of how to live, how else can you ask others to lead you. You are so far from knowing the truth and letting the truth set you free.

Try not to be discouraged. These are the difficult, traumatic times before the New Age. The storm before the calm. I keep saying pray, pray, pray and do not accept second best for yourself or for others. You have a right to good, to health, to joy. Hold your whole planet in the Christ Light, the Light of Good. Truly I tell you it does help. It is more powerful than the people on the planet, it is more powerful than you can imagine, but try to imagine that power, for your own good.

LIFE IN THE NEXT WORLD

I have never read anywhere what our bodies are like at their next stage; we seem to have been impressed with the idea that we will be all ethereal, sort of see-through. Yet I have read someone saying the next world is more solid than this and looking back we seem less solid. I would like to know if we have veins and arteries with blood in, nails that grow, hair that grows. Somewhere I read that we do not need food, but can eat fruit if we wish. Will you please tell me more about all this.

You become much lighter; your substance is different. Compare yourself now with a large oak tree with its trunk and branches, then compare yourself with a sweet pea with its fragile petals and its delicate stem. All have life in them and they all have their own substance. You cannot see what is going on inside the tree as it grows, nor inside the sweet pea. And they cannot see inside you, although they can pick up your thoughts, especially your love. Now visualise a much lighter body, looking similar to you but able to re-assemble itself at will. The soul can raise or lower its vibrations, thus altering its density.

You talk about your life-blood as being your presence, because you do not understand what your soul is. You cannot see it, but we can see your soul and you too will see souls 'in person' when you enter the heaven world.

A flower doesn't appear to sleep; you cannot see it taking in food or moisture, but it is absorbing these. You will absorb what you wish to absorb and you will be able to take in fruit if you choose to, but you will not choose to eat or drink in the way that you do now. Think of a life thread instead of life blood, think of an even atmosphere. You will experience thought transference instead of speech, more harmonious sounds, no loud noises; beautiful colours and sounds that you cannot even dream of from where you are now.

You will understand the no-time, no-space syndrome. You will be both transparent and solid at the same time. It will be to you like wearing a thin summer garment instead of a thick winter coat.

What about hair and nails, and if we don't really eat will we still have teeth?

You can choose how you wish your hair to be, you will find your hands are beautiful, in fact you will be the picture of beauty that you wish to be. Others will see you as you wish them to see you, but remember they will also know all your thoughts. The substance of your teeth and bones and the texture of your flesh will be quite different from now. You will not deteriorate, wear out, get tired, feel hungry, feel cold.

Will there be different skin colours? Yes, I know there will be without asking, and as we re-incarnate so many times I imagine we can choose which 'person' we want to be in the next world. I wonder why I would like to have skin the colour of an Italian. I think our white skins are rather insipid!

Are you criticising my work? No! I am only joking. There is so much you will re-discover. There is a limit as to how much you can understand in your present earthly body.

As no one will eat flesh, will there be cows, pigs and sheep? What would be the point?

The animals might ask what will be the point of having you there who have slaughtered them for your food while on earth! But, yes, there will be all animals and you will see them in the most beautiful surroundings, moving without fear and giving out their love and receiving yours. You will find at-one-ment with many things.

Do we sort of shiver ourselves into the person we want to be recognised us. I mean, if I want to meet all my earthly friends from this present life do I make myself look like the me I am here, then when I want to meet my North American Indian friends, with whom I am sure I have lived in the past, do I shiver myself into looking like I did then?

You are picking up my explanations well. You are remembering. You are re-living some of your other experiences at this moment.

Recall your speed of thought when you answer your telephone (who it may be, what good or bad news there is, even before the caller has spoken) or if you see what you think is an accident going to happen. In less than seconds you have gone through many, many possibilities. That is just an illustration of how different conditions will seem. Remember the ant thinking how far away the rockery is from the pathway; looking on, you can see all at once and know that there is hardly any distance. I think you have enough to think about for now. God bless you, my child.

DROP-OUTS IN HEAVEN

The idyllic life we hear about, know about, on the next plane, which appeals to a large percentage of us, would seem a terrible existence to many young people of today, in fact not only young ones. I am thinking of the vulgar, loud-mouthed, uncouth young and those we call the 'dirty old men'. What happens to them, especially when they pass over quickly and unexpectedly and haven't given any thought to an after-life?

You have read enough to understand you find yourself where you want to be. There is no hurry to get to 'heaven'. I have talked at length in the CWG books about finding out 'Who You Want to Be' and 'Who You Really Are', about 'Waking Up' while on earth. If you do not do that, or bother about that, while on earth, you have the opportunity when you get to the other side. Remember about the Thought and Action syndrome. You can arrive asleep or awake. When you awake you use your imagination, and that is using thought.

Do you think the sort of people you are talking about are really happy?

No, I feel they may think they are, or they just don't know any better.

Jesus said, 'In my Father's House are many Mansions'. You choose where you want to be. It is your choice, you are not made to go to certain 'places'. A goldfish might choose to go into a bowl, then looking out would see how much nicer it appeared in a pond; then a great lake with many other fish might appeal. A chicken might find itself in a small coop because that was all it had known, but it would soon choose freedom in a farmyard or a field of corn. Someone who had lived rough, sleeping on pavements, would be drawn to a little room, be it ever so basic; then they would choose a small flat. That could seem heaven after a pavement.

Now there is something else you might like to consider. Think of the person who has lived in a mansion, with servants, cars, swimming pools, everything he or she thought they desired. He can find himself in something similar, but it has lost its charm, because he was rather lonely and without real friends in his earthly mansion and finds himself in the same position again. Now when he uses his imagination, he longs for real friends, the company of loved ones who have gone on before. He draws to himself or herself something more meaningful, more satisfying. He may wish to meet the painters of some of the pictures he owned on earth, or the makers of some of his beautiful furniture.

A street-player, who played his fiddle with his cap on the ground for coppers, might like to find himself playing a beautiful violin in a wonderful orchestra. Can you begin to imagine the joy of the reality?

Thought, like prayer, is powerful, so powerful. Remember there are those souls around who are longing to help you 'on your way' at whatever level you find yourself, for there is always something better ahead.

There are all the things to experience that are now free. There are Halls of Learning, wonderful scenery the like of which you can only try to imagine while on earth. I am not telling you 'fairy stories', although you know they also have a foundation. There are the 'little people' on earth that some clairvoyants see, and young children see, but others scoff and think they are illusions. Remember, you cannot imagine anything that is not. That gives you much to think about – and you, yourself, have often done this, thought about this.

So your thieves, your murderers, your bullies, your drunks, can think themselves out of their misery. On the other hand, your truly starving, homeless, pitiful souls, who seemingly, through no fault of their own, live in such horror, soon rise above their misery, because, as I told you the other day, many of them chose to come back to earth to bring out your compassion, your thoughtfulness, and their reward is great.

While on earth most of you get your pleasure from material things, but know that is not where true happiness lies. The experience of love, thoughtfulness, kindness, the sound of bird-song, are above all riches. I know what pleases my children before they ask, I know what is in store for them. Seek and you shall find, ask and it will be given to you, knock and it will be opened to you.

I, God, bless you all.

ACCIDENTS

28.2.01

This little Island certainly seems to be going through a bad patch – yet you say, dear God, nothing happens by chance! Are the floods, the Foot & Mouth Disease and now the road and rail disaster all meant to be?

Nothing does happen by chance, there are no accidents. On the physical level you look for material reasons as to why events happen. The floods are caused by your changing weather conditions, the Foot and Mouth Disease is spreading because it is so easily contagious, the road/rail accident happened because of the vehicles veering off the road and there was nothing to stop them careering down on to the railway line just as locomotives were near that spot. Yes, they are the material reasons.

Looked at spiritually, these happenings are causing man to think what he is doing, or not doing, to treat nature with respect. Man is causing his own suffering.

But these things are causing death and pain to innocent people, to those who have had nothing to do with 'nature'.

We talked recently about being 'an accessory after the fact'. You are all passing the buck. Nature didn't cause the floods, the pigs didn't ask for their disease, the vehicles didn't decide to collide. Notice I am not saying the people in the vehicles.

Your old enemy FEAR is playing a very strong part here. The people have become very afraid of flooding, the farmers are terrified about losing their livelihoods, the passengers in cars and trains are afraid of accidents. There are great waves of fear attaching to many conditions.

Surely it is not surprising when so many have experienced, or read about, the floods, diseases, rail and road accidents. I have to call them accidents.

I have told you Thought is so powerful, Fear is so powerful. How many people are praying positively at this time for every train journey to be safe, for every car, and car driver, to be safe, to act safely? How many people think to encase themselves in a globe of golden light as a protection when they go about, either in traffic, in lonely countryside, or at night, in what you call dangerous districts? You, yourself, know that your Guide or your Guardian Angel can be with you in a flash.

When you pray for others, be they unwell, travelling, seemingly over-working, how do you picture your prayer. You believe that a higher being or a Light or Something, surrounds them as a protection. Well, I tell you, that is what happens. You raise their consciousness, or your consciousness of them, or their vibrations, into a Higher Care. If you are someone who prays, then you are someone who believes and you are someone who feels pretty sure your prayers are heard, listened to. You are believing in divine protection and you are right to do so.

Now, you will say, but what about those who are killed in those crashes?

They are not dead, they have gone straight into another dimension. Those who are left behind mourn, but those who have 'passed on' are in a much better place, without having to wait for a later death.

What about those who were injured, particularly those who were badly injured, whose injuries will affect the whole of the rest of their earthly lives?

They have been given the opportunity of learning some wonderful lessons. You do not know, you cannot tell, how that will alter their real selves. The physical injuries may be very serious, but they can cause wonderful spiritual experiences, sometimes wonderful healing experiences between them and their relatives or partners. Do not judge. This is difficult for you all. There are possibilities you do not even dream of.

You all need a lot of faith, belief, understanding, to grasp these truths. It is not easy for you, especially if you have only recently started to think of these things in depth. You cannot run before you can walk. Sometimes, if your walking has been stopped through what you think was an accident, you will learn far more than if you had kept your ability to walk.

This earth life is only temporary. It may seem long while you live it, but when you look back it will be as nothing. You will understand why things happened to you. Many of these things you Chose to happen, although you do not realise.

Sometimes you call people accident-prone. Those people draw trouble to themselves in various ways, sometimes through desire, sometimes through fear, sometimes through thoughtlessness. Those people can learn to protect themselves by affirmations, daily remembering, "I am in God's care all the time, only good can be with me. I proceed in all directions, knowing that I am divinely protected. All is well in my world." If they make a reality of that, really believing what they are saying, and daily repeating it, they will 'wake up' to the fact that they no longer suffer those old seeming accidents.

Pray to me, talk to me, about these things and they will become clearer to you. I give you only Good. Come into my presence, feel it, be conscious of it, love it and know that I am loving you all the time. You are, in reality, never out of my presence, nor can you be for you and I are one.

WHY PRAY FOR OTHERS?

I have just read through what you said yesterday and can understand it up to a point. Now I have a problem in understanding why we pray for others. If there are no accidents or coincidences, praying for another's safety seems pointless, because you say nothing happens that is not meant to happen! This would apply to our own safety too.

You think I am not going to be able to answer this to your satisfaction, don't you?

Well, ...yes.

Remember about Choice? Recall hearing someone say, "I should have been on that train, but my car broke down on the way to the station" or, "I decided not to fly until next week."

Now you ask me, well who would choose to have an accident anyway? So, perhaps they have just decided not to be in an accident. Perhaps they

81

are ready for a different kind of lesson. Your own conscientiousness is making itself heard by you, you have picked up a message from it, or you have picked up the thought of a loved one, and then that is not an accident either. You are learning all the time, you are waking up, you are becoming Who You Want to Be. You can refresh your memory with all this by re-reading the CWG trilogy.

This sounds as if no one had said a prayer for the safety of any of those affected by 'accidents', no one had said a 'safety prayer' for themselves either.

Sometimes a fatal 'accident' happens to one person and the very person next to them is unscathed. Then you often say, all of you, 'it was meant to be'. Yes, nothing happens by Chance. You do not pray by Chance, you do not hold someone 'in the Light' by Chance.

Then it's bad luck for those who don't pray or have anyone to pray for them!

There is nothing to stop them praying for themselves, and including those around them. A prayer can be just a positive thought, a fleeting flash of Good; an almost unconscious thought.

When danger is near and you feel it, your Guide, your Guardian Angel, Me (God) (Good) can be with you in a flash. You have only to call out instantly. You, yourself, know you would do that in an emergency. Good knows no barriers, no time, no space.

This does not mean that because you pray for a sick soul to live, that soul will necessarily go on living. You do not know what is best for others. Hand them over to me and you will have done your very best. You know, yourself, you have learned to do this, and when you do, you experience a feeling of relief. Whereas you had been anxious, you then know a feeling of ease. There is someone else who knows better how to act and that is Me. But I can do this easier through you, you become a direct channel when you find your peace in which to work. There are times when, by looking on, you can be more objective than those who are very close to a situation and who make a thick barrier of fear. They are trying to see through a fog.

Oh, God, you are so clever. I know you are, but you are able to make Me understand and that can't be easy!

We are getting on better, aren't we? You feel more confident. You trust yourself more in putting down what I say.

Do I get it mostly right, for it is so important that I do?

I will not let you misinterpret what I say. The odd word might not matter, but the substance is what matters. You can feel pleased with yourself. You used to put yourself 'down' too much; you were told this. Now you feel worthy, as you should.

Thank you, dear God. Suppose I started putting down my own thoughts and they were not right, would you just stop coming through me?

Your thoughts are my thoughts and my thoughts are your thoughts. But I tell you this, if you did not 'tune-in' sincerely, you would experience a blank when you asked for help. You know now that sometimes you have to wait several minutes before you 'hear'. You are just not quite on 'key', no pun meant!

We have never yet had such a light-hearted bit of conversation! I feel quite bouncy!

OUR FOOD SUPPLY

4.3.01

The news of the Foot & Mouth Disease gets worse; it is spreading out of control. Part of me is hoping it is the beginning of the ending of eating animals and birds, for a start has to be made somewhere. Then I think of all the desperate farmers, watching their years of work being destroyed in front of them and their anxiety for their livelihoods. What are they to do? How can they best be helped?

Keep holding on to your positive thoughts. You are not the only one praying for animals to be spared and vegetarianism to become the normal diet of humans. You have no idea how many of my children are praying at this time for a change to take place for the better.

When there is a shortage of meat, people will find they can live without it. Adventurous farmers will change over to arable farming and the growing of vegetables and fruits. Yes, it will take what you would call 'a long time' to grow suitable protection-hedges for cultivating the needs of different species of trees and bushes and plants. It takes a long time to work out how to reach the moon and it costs a lot of money, but ways and means are found and isn't your food supply more important than reaching other planets?

The sooner a start is made, the better. Times will seem hard initially, but some help has been promised to farmers from your government. As I have said earlier, and in other books, if you stopped making armaments there would be a lot more money to help the unemployed, let alone the starving and homeless.

Pray for your land, literally for your land. With right and thoughtful treatment it can feed and keep you. Delicious, healthier food can be grown without harming your brother animals, without adversely affecting your ecology.

What about the road hauliers and the butchers and the animal markets? Those posts must employ as many people as farming?

There is work for all. Try to stop thinking about, even considering, lack. Shops can sell other items than meat, lorries can carry other goods than animals and carcasses. A better way can always be found if it is looked for in the right places, with the right motives.

You say there is no right and wrong.

I am using those words differently here. Just read through and you will understand that sometimes there needs to be a contradiction because of your limited speech, your limited words. Do not look for trouble where none is intended. Keep to the positive, the constructive, the better way, in all things. You can diversify, you can innovate, you can Change for the better. You can progress. Surely progress is what you all desire? You want for things to be better, but notice I do not say bigger in this instance. You have lost the wonderful flavours in many of your fruits and vegetables through interfering with their nature.

What harm is being done with trying to alter genes, with genetic engineering?

Sometimes man learns the 'hard way'. He pays dearly for his mistakes. He does not listen to his inner knowing, his conscience. We have talked about all this before under the heading of GREED. Not greed for food, but greed for money. That old bugbear, money.

If only you would remember to be satisfied, to be peaceful, to trust, to stop your rushing for 'jam today'.

So the most help we, the on-lookers, can give to the farmers, the hauliers, the tradesmen, is to 'hold them in the Light of Supply, of Good, knowing that alternatives will be found for them because they are all in YOUR care all the time.

Many ways are running through your mind on how to get this message across, of how to spread this advice. Then a fear creeps in that the message will not only be met with ridicule, but those who could spread it, your ministers, your clergy, your teachers, will be afraid to speak out. You need to start somewhere. Sitting back, looking on, doing nothing, is getting you all nowhere. Act, have faith, believe, pray. Be vigilant for openings that will present themselves for putting forward right thoughts, good thoughts, practical thoughts. Remember about 'seeing' the end product, then making it work, then thinking about it. That reverse order from that which you are used to using. You know it works.

COMMUNICATION WITH ALL LIVING THINGS

6.3.01

I have just been for a country walk. It was cold but sunny and so worthwhile having made the effort to walk. The bulbs were peeping through in the cottage gardens and the birds were chirping. I spoke to some ducks. This made me wonder how do birds think? Is it all just instinct with them or do they 'talk' to each other?

I was with you on that walk. You did a lot of thinking and a little bit of regretting. All is always well in your world at each particular moment. You can look back and you can look forward, but all is NOW. Live in each moment.

To answer your question. All Life lives by instinct. You, yourself, know when you are tired, when you are hungry, when you are sleepy, when you are cold, hot, happy, sad. You do many things automatically, without thinking in actual words. Animals live by instinct. They too 'feel' cold, heat, hunger, joy; yes, joy. Most animals, meaning fish and birds and all mammals, like company, as most of you do. They have a strong mating instinct, but they are quite particular about who they mate with.

Does this apply to insects?

You would be very surprised how sensitive insects are. Some like to live in great colonies, others can survive in isolation. The basic need of all life, as you know it, is food.

As for communication; you hear birds calling to each other, usually for a mate or to a mate; you hear dogs answering another bark. You can communicate with all other forms of life and it is usually through love and patience. All life has sensitivity and susceptibility and this includes plant life. Remember how the trees loosened their roots, ready for removal, at Findhorn? Some had been told they were going to be moved. When another tree nearby was put to the test it had not loosened its roots.

Is all this to do with getting on the right wave-lengths, the right vibrations of other life forms?

It is first to do with love for one another, then lower vibrations can rise and higher vibrations can lower. Do you understand?

Yes. You always make things seem so easy to understand. How do I know this is not just me thinking for myself? Well, of course I know it is not, for I am not clever enough!

Here we go again. You are doubting. You are not remembering that you and I are one and that my thoughts are your thoughts. Why don't you communicate with that pheasant?

[This bird had been annoying me and my neighbours for weeks, running amok through our gardens, pecking shoots and screeching.]

Well, I sort of tried, but it is not friendly. It seems vicious. It is making itself a nuisance.

Wouldn't you try to make yourself a nuisance if you were looking for food and had learned that other species could supply it? Haven't you made yourselves a 'nuisance' to my sheep, chickens, cows, fish?

Yes, that makes me rather ashamed. We have used our strength and force upon your creatures. We have taken fish out of water and let them gasp in air, we have frightened livestock in many, many ways, all for the sake of our stomachs.

We didn't finish our conversation about communication between birds. Do they enjoy each others' bird-song and do they actually chatter meaningfully?

You do a lot of chatter, you communicate with vocal noise, but you also communicate your feelings in many other ways. Not just with your thoughts, but with your actions, your facial expressions, your body expressions, your movements. Those two strong words I keep telling you about, Love and Fear, communicate without words. Why would that be only between humans? Why not apply that to animals, birds, fish, insects? Think about this.

Yes, I will, I want to read what I have written, but I must learn more while I am through to you. I know I can always get through, but today I don't want to stop yet. What would you like to communicate to me, dear God?

You are learning, remembering, all the time, whether you are in direct contact like this, or just doing your thinking. You are seeing more in everything that is going on around you, with your connection to all things, with your contacts with other people and particularly your friends.

You are experiencing how affirmations work, how prayer works. You are not wasting your 'time' on so much useless thought, useless wanting. You are learning to be constructive in all your dealings. You are absorbing much more from your reading, your serious reading. But earth life is not all serious, enjoy all the fun which I put there for your 'entertainment'. Lightness comes with laughter. You can turn all negative into positive, all sadness into joy, all anger into understanding. One of your sons did just that and he has seen the good, positive results. Disharmony has turned into harmony. Nobody got 'hurt', only briefly. He was an example to others as well as to himself.

Oil takes longer to spread than water. Many of you are pouring oil on troubled waters. Know that all is happening for the best, to make my children remember, to be more caring. Times of great need bring out the compassion in my children. Nothing good is wasted.

The troublesome pheasant has disappeared, gone! After several weeks. I did "speak" to him or her several times through the window, and without malice, telling it this was not the right place for it. To go off and find mates over in the fields. It worked!!

* * *

87

Having read the CWG Trilogy three times, I have now nearly finished reading Book 3 for the fourth time. That book seemed difficult to grasp initially, now it seems mostly easy to understand.

I suppose I have learned much in the intervals and I have now 'talked' to you, dear God, at length. Your words lift me up, give me great hope and make me happy. Then I listen to so-called 'intellectuals' pontificating on the radio or television and I wonder how ever long it will be before they stop and listen to themselves. They sometimes appear to me to be talking a lot of self-satisfied nonsense.

This Foot and Mouth Disease is ruffling so many feathers and extending far beyond the livelihoods of the affected farmers. When listening to an interesting programme on TV recently, there was just one vegetarian on the podium and she was ridiculed so loudly, treated as if she were an ignorant fool. Few in the audience seemed to be on her wavelength, yet she kept her cool. It is then that I feel what a long way we have to travel before we get our ideas right, listened to, heeded.

I have been thinking that it is like telling a smoker to quit smoking, how bad it is for him or her, what a silly habit it is, how unpleasant it is for non-smokers, etc. The smokers will always come up with what they consider good reasons, plausible excuses, for carrying on. Then it is the same with alcoholics, drug addicts. Now I begin to see that is where they want to be. They have chosen, with their free choice, to do or think their way.

It makes me understand better why you keep saying in that trilogy about finding out Who We Want to be, What We Want to be.

Good seems such a drop in the ocean of Bad, yet you say there is no right and wrong, no good and bad. We mostly walk about with our eyes and ears closed, our minds taken up with such mundane things, such trivialities. Being an Aries, things don't work quickly enough for my liking!

Although I am longing to 'get on to the other side' I also wish I were much younger so that I had more time here to try to make more impression 'on your behalf'.

I am alone much of my time, yet I am never lonely because I know you are with me and much fills my mind. However, I truly miss deep conversation.

We can learn much from listening to others who are deep thinkers. Also, I miss the company and nearness of my sons and of Carol and Linda and Sue. I like living on my own, yet I want human warmth and hugs. This sounds unkind to my wonderful friends, yet they mainly do not give me – do I mean depth?

Anyway, you know better than anyone, dear God, how I am feeling – such a drop in the ocean, such a minute helper for a better world. We are so far from living in our Peace, our inheritance, our Oneness. I have all I need, yet something is missing, something important, and I suppose I don't really know what it is. Unless it is the thought of what is to come. I will be patient meanwhile for I know that my time of going is not yet. This work I embarked on must be spread around – and anyway my beloved garden will very shortly need my full attention in an effort to make it as beautiful as I can.

* * *

To my readers:

Do I hear you thinking 'how dare this woman say, or even think, she is talking to God'? I can quite understand that. I asked myself the same question many times initially.

Then I realise that as (not if) I am God's perfect child whom he loves, why shouldn't He and I communicate. Surely that is the safest way to find the Truth and to be able to pass on the Truth to you.

Much of my time and speech (when I have not 'tuned-in') is not as God's perfect child, but that is my problem. At those times I am not portraying my Maker as I should. 'Maker' – that is an old-fashioned sounding word for God, but how true it is. He did make us and he is interested in our every thought and action.

As I said earlier, you do not have to read this and it is up to you whether you 'feel' it is right. What can you put forward that seems more truthful, easier to understand, just as much in line with what is taking place on our planet?

Exciting improvements are on the horizon. Ford Motors have just spent millions on creating a car that can run on hydrogen – and the exhaust is fit to drink! Let us hold that idea "in the Light", let us picture it happening, make a reality of it for the sake of our planet.

Then in CWG (Book 3) I read what a wonderful commodity hemp is. Now, only this week, I watched a house being built with it, after the hemp had been treated in a certain and safe way. Other uses were mentioned. Are we listening at last? Let us all find out more about these wonderful 'discoveries'.

It quite literally hurts to see the thousands of sheep and cattle being stunned and burned at this time. How terrified they must be, smelling death all around them. And our hearts go out to the farmers who have cared for them. But is it not an opportunity to stop replacing those animals? A start to growing food for vegetarians – growing corn, nuts, fruits, vegetables, in their place? Of course it will take time, but a start has to be made and the sooner the better.

I once thought vegetarians were a bit cranky and I still cannot cope with vegans. Having now been a vegetarian for twenty years or more, I cannot bear the sight of dead flesh in the shops and supermarkets. Raw meat filled with blood. If you think there is not sufficient nourishment for your body without eating dead, bloody flesh, read some books and statistics about vegetarianism. It is certainly an eye-opener – unless you read with your eyes shut, determined to think it is rubbish!

How I regret forcing one of my sons to eat meat against his will when he was very young. He was a 'natural' vegetarian and I turned him into a meat-eater because I thought he needed it.

Dear Ones, keep an open mind. Pray for wisdom. There is a big difference between believing and knowing. Mary Baker Eddy, the Christian Science Founder, said, "it is no use a captain believing his ship will not sink if there is a hole in it."

* * *

Dear God, why, oh why, are we living so much longer and why are the medical profession so adamant about keeping us alive, prolonging our lives when we might have slipped peacefully away? Our hospitals are overflowing with poor old souls looking hopeless, helpless, sometimes behaving in an insane way, not knowing who they are.

You mean 'why are you living on your earth plane so much longer' for you never stop living. You know that. If you stop using your body, it becomes stiff and weak, when you stop using your minds they become blank, not open to more learning. Sometimes these are the reasons for an inability to stay agile and creative. Remember you create each minute of your life.

You have the ability to know when it is time for you to drop off the 'old coat'; instead you use your power to cling on, to cling on to your material life, your material possessions, your family.

Learn, remember, to let go all the time, not to keep items that have lost their usefulness. Apply this to your homes, your possessions. Let go of the clutter. Then it will be easier for you to let go of the worn out coat. You will not need that coat in your next home. You will see your family again, you will meet your family again. You will look on at your earth family and you will meet your family that has gone on before. Is that not a comforting thought? You will be loved, you will feel wonderful.

Start to picture what you wish your heaven to be like, knowing that it can be just like that, when you leave the earth plane. You prepare in advance for a holiday, yet you rarely think about your return 'home'. You know it is there, but some of you are afraid to return because you are not remembering how lovely it was when you left it to return to earth.

The clinging on affects so many other people. It worries the family; they feel guilty if they cannot be of much use. We fill up those hospital beds needed by others, much younger. Is all this because of a deep-rooted fear of death?

Here you have a situation where you both fear death yet you know deep down there is nothing to fear. You know you, yourself, have been able to say "Go on, go on, they are all awaiting you", but when you wanted to say that recently to one you loved, her daughter indicated No! No!

91

It is not only those who are sick who cling on, it is often those who are on-lookers who are clinging on. All this is Fear and a lack of understanding of what is happening.

You know that I have always felt it is wrong to keep people alive by artificial means, yet I was dead against euthanasia. Now I think euthanasia would be kind when people's minds have gone awry, when they have no quality of life. Would euthanasia be so wrong? We put our pets out of their misery, not easily, but with love. We are slaughtering thousands of your animals. Where is right and wrong, of which you say there is neither?

When all my children realise there is no death, they will think and act differently. Choose to know what is best, what is kindest. Choose to become more enlightened. Choose to be very thoughtful over this situation. You have free choice, but you also have guidance at your side.

In all cases of doubt, nay at all times, Pray, Pray for Guidance and enlightenment. Good is with you at all times, use it, use Me.

SUDDEN DEATH

What is your message to those who have lost dear ones, but have no body to bury? That seems to concern them so much and I try to put myself in their position.

Firstly, they have not 'lost' their dear ones. There is no separation. Life goes on and on, there is no before and after. It matters not that the outgrown coat cannot be buried or burned, the soul that it covered is free. Think of a bird that flies up into the sky – it has left behind its nest or the bush it was resting on – and it is experiencing a wonderful sense of freedom, to fly where it wishes. Yes, in this instance it still has its 'body' with it, but experience the sense of freedom. Sometimes it flies out of sight, but you know it is still 'somewhere'.

Yes, I can picture this and it is a lovely picture, but I hear the parent, the partner, the child, saying, 'but I didn't say "Goodbye", I didn't prove to myself that the soul had departed, that it had left its body'.

What you are really saying is that you did not see 'it' dead. I tell you, it is not dead. Do try to remember that it is not dead. You will not be dead, ever. You will leave your present earth plane at some time, but you will not be un-alive. You will be experiencing the most wonderful freedom that you have felt since you left your 'real' home. You will be flying directly back 'home' and others will be guiding you, loving you, there for you. Dear Ones, let go of the blackness, the black ties, the black clothes, the solemn atmosphere.

Of course you are sad, but that is for yourself. Be glad for the flight of your beloved.

When your period of grief subsides, you will feel peace for yourself and for that loved one. Send them your love and your thoughts, speak of them to others. Look forward to a re-union when that time comes, for come it will. Try to lose the thought of space and distance. Think instead of a thin layer of silk or net or cloud between earth and what you call heaven – for that is all it is.

Thank you, dear God. I have known this for a long time and when anniversaries come round I 'link' with my mother or my husband or a special friend and I give them a great big bouquet of flowers; I choose the kind of flowers and the colours I know they liked best and I give it to them with all my love and a hug. I can easily make a reality of it and the feeling is great.

And you know, you do not have to limit it to a bouquet. It can be a wonderful garden that you meet in. You can wander around, recalling great happiness and you can call others to you and have a party! Remember about the power of Thought and the power of true Love. And when you 'part' again you know it is just temporarily.

Now you can visualise how those on 'this side' can come back to you, bringing love and comfort. They want you to know how happy they are, how they look forward to greeting you when your present earth session is completed, or suspended.

I have learned that we are so surprised to find ourselves without blemish, bones in perfect alignment, eyesight perfect, hearing perfect, no aches and pains. The first book that started me thinking like this was Air Chief Marshal Lord Dowding's "Lychgate" and it meant so much to me that I bought a second copy in case I lost one!

My children, you are created to be happy. I have told you before, you cannot get away from Me and I am always with you. You usually turn to me more in times of despair, sorrow, fright, grief. Try turning to me at all times for it will add another dimension to your life.

All this is wonderful, but I still feel so sorry for parents, particularly mothers, who lose children. Also for young lovers who are parted at the height of their happiness. Is there a special message for them?

It really is the same message. There is no death, no separation. They will 'meet' again. They will love again, they will care again. They will understand why a temporary parting happened. And at the re-union it will be as though it had not happened. No time, no space.

I am always with you, my children.

LOOKING AFTER OUR BODY

We may be living a lot longer on this earth plane, but we do seem to be getting an awful lot of complaints – viruses, heart attacks, tuberculosis returning, depression, terminal illness. Are we learning something important from all this?

You could be learning a lot from all this. Mainly you choose to imagine you know most of the answers, the reasons, the treatments.

I would like you to imagine a large, blank sheet of paper. Now know that you are going to design a wonderful house. It can be what size you wish, but it needs to be perfect in every way. It must be damp proof, wind proof, light and airy, yet able to stand up to severe storms. The correct size is necessary for all the items you are going to add in each room. The heating and cooling systems must be perfect. There need to be inlet and outlet pipes. The whole system of heating and lighting needs to be ecologically kind. There needs to be storage space, a perfectly operating temperature control; an alarm system. You can add other items so long as they do not interfere with or adversely affect other people.

Now when this house materialises you see how perfect your plan is. You choose to live in it.

To start with all seems well. Then you become a bit careless with it, knocking it about a bit, but not enough to make much difference. Then you go away for a holiday and you forget to shut the windows against adverse weather conditions. Never mind, you think, it will dry out again. I will add extra heat.

Then the fuel runs low and you ignore the warning sign. Never mind, you will order a bit extra. The sun shines too brightly for your liking through some of the windows, it affects your television screen, so you decide to shut out all the light on that particular wall. Now you have cured one thing, but you don't much like the gloom you have caused. You will add high wattage bulbs that really light up that particular room. Oh dear, the current was too much for the cable and all the fuses blew. An electrician suggests you put in a new system.

You think you would like to alter the colour schemes. Somehow your new ideas make the whole place look different. Some rooms are now so gloomy you feel depressed so you ask your physician for some anti-depressant tablets

Because you have poured too much bulky waste down the plug hole in the sink, it blocks up. Instead of changing your habits, you pour down strong, harmful chemicals to dissolve the trouble.

The walls begin to show cracks, but instead of letting in more air and causing more ventilation, you fill up the holes with a new kind of filler. Having spent a small fortune on filler, you are disappointed to see it does not bond with the original materials. Never mind, there will be another kind of filler to try.

And so on and so on. You know where I am heading, don't you?

What you do now is to apply this to the perfect blueprint that your body was at its beginning. How did you treat it? Did you abuse it? Were you dissatisfied with it? Did you try to 'improve' it?

Did you ever stop to think perhaps the original design could not be improved upon? Would it not have been better to be grateful for what you had originally? Did you put too much stress and strain on the framework, too much grease and not enough fine oil on the joints? Have you overloaded the finely tuned computer? Is it now suffering from stress?

Do think about how you are treating your beautiful bodies. They are a miracle of perfection and deserve to be treated with the utmost care and consideration and respect. It pays to be grateful and give thanks for a beautiful house – do the same with your bodies.

You are concerned, my child, that today you have written this analogy instead of Me! Well, you have, but as usual I was guiding you and we can smile together at the result!

6.4.01

I have been thinking about secrets. When they are personal ones they are usually because we do not want someone else to know something; we fear what they might think of us. Only sometimes is the reason unselfish so that another is saved from worry or sadness. Then I think about international secrets and realise how dangerous they are. We, or they, have discovered or made some ghastly item of destruction. We want to keep the knowledge to ourselves so that we have a means of annihilating another country or countries, or as a means of defending ourselves.

This has come to me particularly now because of the United States plane, full of secret knowledge, that has inadvertently landed on a Chinese island. This has caused suspicion, fear, antagonism, distrust and the possibility of a 'cold war' developing. All because of Secrets which should not exist were we to live in our Peace, satisfied with our own piece of the planet. You have explained about this kind of situation earlier, but will you please din it into us again.

Oh, if only you could all grow up. You can see 'your rose' fully open and being blown in all directions. It cannot be in all places at once, not while it is tossed hither and thither, but it CAN be in all places at once as a beautiful opening bud.

When one nation is brave enough to say 'No more wars, no more weapons, no more SECRETS. We will be the first to be the most wonderful example for the beginning of a perfect world'. That will be a commencement. Choose for this to happen, choose for other nations to follow that great example. Choose to know that the Peace you give out will be returned to you.

What would be the point of trying to overcome a nation if there were no resistance? How could revenge, or hate work if it met no resistance; if it met only love and forgiveness. If you kept hitting someone and they just gave out love and more love in return, you would feel defeated; you would feel a bit silly; you would wonder why you were fighting and for what. You would run away.

You would want to return home, for it is natural to wish to live in your familiar surroundings, especially when you found them getting better and better. This would happen because all the wealth that had been wasted on armaments and armies would be spent on improvements all over the world.

When you remember the wonder of where you have come from – that other world to which you will all return – you will want to experience it here and now. Other nations would look on, envious, unbelieving, yet with a great urge to try it out for themselves. Who is going to be first to make, to take, this great big step for peace and happiness to become normal, every-day existence?

Choose to give up FEAR. You find it so difficult to do that. You choose to live in fear of each other instead of love for each other. Choose to share your Peace, your love, your very life and all good will come to you, pushed down and running over. My children, Highly Evolved Beings look upon you with disbelief that you can be so uncivilised.

When you give up your fight for what is not yours, you will find time to communicate with others for the good of the whole. You will find how unnecessary it is to mis-treat your land, your bodies, your forests, your atmosphere. When you share your SECRETS it will be for the benefit of all life. You will find so much joy in sharing your discoveries, your improvements. You will know a joy few of you have experienced for centuries. Who is brave? Who is strong? Who is Fearless? Who is selfless enough and trusting enough to put into practice what you know in your hearts makes sense?

Pray, choose, think deeply. It is your choice as to whether you stay as very little children or start to grow into the wonderful adults that, as a child, you wanted to be.

SUICIDE

19.4.01

Yesterday, Esther Rantzen's TV programme was about suicide. She had bereaved parents on the panel and in the audience and some young people who had attempted suicide. The grief and guilt was so terribly sad. How I wished I could comfort those people – tell them there is no death, implore them not to feel so guilty. I think people who take their own lives are incredibly brave. Is it wrong of me to think that?

Just as great pain can become too much to bear, then you pass out, so too can earth life sometimes seem too much to bear and you choose to give up. It is your choice, that is why you are neither condemned nor punished.

It can seem selfish, yes, because you did not think of the agony you were going to cause those who truly love you. Those left 'behind' do not understand and they think you are lost to them forever. The parting is only temporary.

Now I am not suggesting that it is OK to kill yourself without much thought. Is it right for you to be running away from your circumstances? Are you neglecting to learn or remember a great lesson here? You are never without help and advice. Materially you heard yesterday of all the organisations that are there to help you in your distress. Alternatively, you can speak to Me. Yes, talk to me as you would to another human being, not as a God to be in awe of. All you have to do is to ask for strength and guidance as to what you could be doing. I am your best friend.

If you take that final earthly step yourself, you will not be killing yourself, for that is not possible. You will just be moving from one dimension to another. Instead of releasing yourself from your trauma, you may find yourself just looking on and wishing you had not hurried on your 'transfer'. You took an early flight instead of waiting for the one scheduled for you.

If your life seems unbearable, Choose for it to change. Choose for what you wish to experience. Mountains can become as mole-hills as well as the other way round. You are never without an understanding friend – even if it is ONLY ME!.

As I so often say, I am here – USE ME.

PREDICTIONS

I should like to ask you about Annie Kirkwood's book, "Mary's Message to the World". I lent it to a friend recently and she thought it 'rather fanciful'. I think it is wonderful and I like to think it is the truth, but many of the forecast dates have proved to be wrong.

Notice how you are fidgeting! You think I am not going to answer this to your satisfaction, don't you?

Forgive me, yes.

Everything happens 'at the right time' – time not necessarily being a particular hour or date in your sense of time. Did you go out last Tuesday, or was it Wednesday, and was it 3 o'clock or 4 o'clock? Does it now really matter? Are you going out next week on a certain day, at a certain time? Does it really matter?

Yes, you say, because it may be to catch a plane or meet a friend at a station. But are not those plane and train times frequently altered? The plane and the train are the same vehicles, or similar ones. There is no time nor space, but you remain the same person, the same entity, who is going to meet another 'same' entity.

Mary's Message is mainly a true message of the past and a true request for you all to pray, to be vigilant, to care, really care, for your planet, as she does. My Son, Jesus, added his own message at the end of the book. These writings are there to help you all.

When people read your autobiography, do they ask you if every detail is exactly true? You believe it is, but you rely on your earthly memory, so minute details may be slightly incorrect, but it does not alter the story.

You are also wondering how much is true of the current TV story "Son of God". That is partly composed by research, partly by excavations and partly by memory. Yes, memory.

And how do you feel when you watch the strife and unrest that it going on in those same Eastern cities at this present time? Has there been progress? Would you like to walk about out there today? Each Country thinks it is right, doing the right thing, yet all that is being experienced is fear and greater fear. Those people are so far from being happy.

Yes, there is truth in much of what you see, what you hear, what you read. Be discerning and thoughtful in all things.

There is only one way, one simple way, to God. That is in your hearts, in your remembrance. You do not need to fight for a certain way to be followed to reach the Great Intelligence, of which you are all part.

You cannot find your Peace while you are greedy, selfish, warring, making up the rules as you go. The Truth is so simple.

I love you all. My wish is that you find your Peace, that you come to me at all times. Amen, Amen, Amen.

Thank you, dear God. A great Peace comes over me when you talk to me like this. God bless you, yourself, may you feel as wonderful as I think you do, and much more besides.

Will you please explain to me about numerology and astrology.

You have just 'seen' your rose fully open and looking in all directions, including upwards.

This is a symbol of how man is ever looking for, seeking, more knowledge. Just as some people find interest in engineering, others in music, there are those who seek to learn more from the stars and from numbers.

There is knowledge to be gained in these subjects for those who genuinely seek Truth. Not everyone wants to know how chemistry works, nor physics; not all of you wish to know about star-gazing and numerology.

Yes, it is true that you are influenced by the position of the stars at your birth. And if you were born 'early' or 'late' you were still under the appropriate influences.

I have just heard that the zodiac signs may have been miscalculated by us and that we should take off a sign, putting us under the previous one. That makes a fallacy of me saying "I am a typical Aries" and thinking that a certain friend of mine is a typical Scorpio!

Wait a minute. Who is saying the zodiac is wrongly placed? How much is in a name? How much research is necessary to prove this new idea? I would say – wait and see.

As to numerology, this is a similar code. Some of you 'know your lucky number or numbers'. How much weight do you give to those predictions and might not 'choosing' come into this? Your study will not help you win the Lottery, but if you find it interesting, then study it. Otherwise, study something else that you can more easily understand. These phenomena will become clearer to you on higher planes.

Is there any point in people trying to arrange certain events to fit in with their zodiacal signs, or on specific dates that are supposed to be lucky or unlucky for them?

Remember about Choice? Remember about Free Will? Nothing happens by chance, whether it be the date of your wedding or the date of your starting a new career. In your heart you have made a Choice and whether, on that special day, the sun shines or there is a terrific storm, that will have been your choice, or the choice of someone else for themselves (not for you).

You know, my children, you do waste a lot of time on items that are not life-threatening, not mega important. Would it not be better if you spent that time in going through the files in your Being and chucking out what is not needed, and re-reading what is helpful?

Being willing to change is therapeutic; it can be a mighty advancement. You carry about a lot of unnecessary clutter. How much of it do you use? Ask yourself 'Do I really need to cling on to this?' 'Will I ever use that, not having used it for the last five years?'

I can't help adding, how many times do we chuck out something, after years of non-use, only to be in a situation where it is just what we need?

And I know what you call that! But you remember only those occurrences and you forget the other times when you have not wanted what you have thrown out.

When you learn that you really do have all you need – I am not saying 'want' – you will be much more content. You cannot bring your possessions with you when you 'die'. You would feel very silly if you did! All you need, or ever wished for, will be yours as soon as you 'think' it. Remember about Thought? You, yourself, have all you need now, yet it is less than half what it used to be. Do you miss anything? No, because you have found more satisfying items, thoughts, people. Being satisfied and content is the first big step towards knowing your Peace, your Divinity.

Bless you all, my children.

PRAYING

What percentage of Christians pray?

It depends what you mean by pray.

I get it! As I pictured the pink rose to focus my mind, the bud opened a little and, for the first time, I could see two shades of pink. Immediately I knew, from the paler outer pink to the deeper inner pink, you were showing me there are different depths of prayer.

Yes, there are many who pray 'on the surface'; they feel a kind of compulsion to pray, to use set prayers, especially the Lord's Prayer. They often do not understand to whom they pray. There is a forlorn hope that they are praying to 'something' that will help them; come to their aid.

Then there are those who pray very sincerely and seriously; those who know God hears them and approves of what they are endeavouring to do.

Lastly, there are the few who talk to Me, knowing, without doubt, that their prayers reach me. They have a good idea of what goes on, but they do not expect to hear me answer. They look for a result, but they do not listen for an answer.

It is when you realise that we, you and I, them and Me, are in true communication, that a bond is made.

Very few hold a two-way conversation with me, knowing that I am with them, at all times, and giving my full attention to listening to what I already know.

We are all ONE, there is no separation. When you telephone a friend they will either answer the phone, or not, according to whether they are in or out. Now the difference here is that I am NEVER OUT! I always answer my telephone line to you and you can always hear my answer. You can train yourselves to hear, to listen.

I do not make choices for you, but I guide you and cause you to think. When you ask for my help I do not ignore you. I suggest solutions to you. You find yourself thinking along a new path or a different path to solve your query.

And I tell you something; I love to hear your soul-voice, to feel your love, and experience your sense of appreciation; appreciation for every little thing in your lives, be it warmth, flowers, friends, equipment that enables you to do your work. Treat me as the most loving, caring friend you could possibly have, who wishes you nothing but good and health and happiness.

You are made of love so it is easy for you to express love, not only to Me but to all things around you, whether it be friends, trees or the food you eat. To be thankful, to be grateful, to be kind, to be loving, fills you with an ecstasy that nothing else can. Unless you are in touch with Me you are only half alive, so to speak.

I have indicated to you earlier how to pray. You communicate with me in the quietness of your Being. You tune-in. Try not to adopt a 'poor me' attitude. That only pulls you down, depresses you, leads you nowhere. Voice your troubles to me briefly – I already know all the details. Now you have created a line of communication. Now ask – and it shall be answered. Then listen and it will be shown to you. Recall much of what the Master Jesus said. He has left you so much, yet it is so simple. Knock, Ask,

Receive. Have not just Faith, but Belief. Believe that I am with you – always.

Then begin to 'see' how your prayers for Good and for your Planet, can be multiplied. Do keep remembering that great Power of Thought. It is Mighty.

Remember that although it may seem only a small proportion who truly knows how to pray, millions of you all over the world are learning, remembering, how to pray, helped tremendously by Neale Donald Walsch's "Conversations with God".

Think of the snowball effect of Neale's first jottings on his yellow lawyer's pad. The result was a trilogy that is now printed in millions in over twenty languages. Now you begin to get an answer to your original question.

Your planet needs your prayers desperately. They can save it from annihilation. They can hasten the healing process. There is so much to heal – the soil, the forests, the atmosphere, the thoughts of all souls.

You can come here, in your dream-state, and look on at your planet. It will give you hope, but it will also devastate your being to see how you are devastating your earth.

Dear Ones, if you love Me, if you love your earth, if you love yourself, pray, pray, pray. Your understanding will open up and you will be enabled to do so much good. You do not need to feel helpless, just an onlooker. You can be a DOER, Choose to be that.

BODILY HARM

If I ask you what you feel or think about boxing and wrestling, you will surely say you have no opinion because you do not judge and we have free will. Am I right in that assumption?

The rose cannot move – it has been knocked out!

Touché! Because as soon as I pictured the rose it was a tight bud and slightly withered. It has never looked like that before!

There is nothing, no thing, to stop you mutilating your bodies. Some of you choose to knock them about, some choose to tattoo their skin, to pierce themselves in many and curious places. Is there pleasure in that? Yes?

I can't think of anything more futile; I cannot begin to understand where the pleasure is and there is surely no pleasure for the onlooker – yet there must be, for these people draw the crowds.

Man's great love of money comes into some of these things. The obscene, the horrific, the oddity, the unusual, come into this. Some men enjoy warfare. Some men find great achievement in designing weapons of destruction. Engine designers try to find ways of making vehicles that go at ever greater speeds. All this is sensationalism. Some of these people we are talking about would not find any sensationalism or emotion in reading great poems, watching wonderful dancing, listening to marvellous music or feeling ecstatic love.

I begin to see that evolvement is portrayed here. What do Highly Evolved Beings (HEBs) think when they look on at some of our "entertainment"?

Multiply what you feel by a hundred thousand and you will begin to feel what they do. You are uncivilised, immature.

There, you do sometimes judge!

I am not giving a judgment. I am stating facts. If you hold a beautiful rose in one hand and in the other you hold one that has been trampled underfoot, you would not see them as equal, as both beautiful. But you would know that the one that had been trampled upon was basically and originally perfect, that more perfect ones were to follow, that the whole bush had not been ravaged.

How do you feel about someone like Ellen MacArthur or Kate Aidie or Nelson Mandela?

They have great strength, great courage. They prove themselves to be great, either to themselves, with no fear, or for the sake of others. They are beginning to be evolved.

Does that mean as we become HEBs (Highly Evolved Beings) we have to be able to perform great acts of bravery, beyond, far beyond, what most of us can do now?

You have just as much choice as HEBs as you do now, but you have learned how to use your choices to their best advantage and for the best advantage of all others. You do not all choose to be great singers, or all choose to be athletic, or all choose to be mechanically minded. And remember there is no competition as such. You are not trying to outdo each other. All is done in love. Your wish is to be way-showers, to encourage others. You have no desire to outshine another, rather you wish their light to be as bright as yours.

Suppose a boxer, a wrestler, a gold-digger (in both senses of the word) wishes to go on doing those things after his earthly death, where does he go?

We come back to your Choice. You, yourself, know that you are not going to sit on a pink cloud, playing a harp, nothing would bore you more. So these people of whom you speak, do not have to 'do' anything that will not please them. They can return to your earth-plane as many times as they like, as most of you have done already. If they do not evolve to a higher level, a higher aspiration, they can choose to remain as they are, or even to go to less evolved civilisations – which I have mentioned exist, in other writings.

Those of you who leave your earth bodies in a very sick state do not choose to re-inhabit that form because they experience the joy of a better Being. All is choice. Each to his or her own.

I think I have trodden on risky ground today, insinuating that there are those who practise unevolved pursuits. Who am I to judge?

You are not judging in that sense of the word. You are not condemning. You feel in your innermost that you have found a happier way of living. Some of those of whom you speak would pity you, think there were no thrills in your life, but you would just go on knowing that was not so.

Where should we 'draw the line' over things that affect our bodies adversely or offend other people? I imagine that watching cruel sport activates the wrong emotions in some others; damaging bodies causes doctors and hospitals to give up time on repairs that should not have been necessary.

How about all the people that are causing your hospitals to be full through having polluted your atmosphere, poisoned your soil, causing much bodily harm? Are they to be blamed less? What a long list you could all make of 'do's' and 'don'ts'. And what a long time – in your idea of time – it is going to take to 'mend' all these ways.

Do not be discouraged. More souls than you realise are working for a far better Life. They are being guided, because they are open to guidance.

But you cannot open the eyes of those determined to keep them tightly closed.

I find it hard to understand how you can look on and not feel devastated with your children and how they are hurting themselves. As parents we really hurt when we see our children suffer.

I know the grass is greener on the other side of the wall. I know that perfection is there for all. I know you will all remember to walk upright, with joy in your hearts and with beautiful smiles on your faces. I do not have to accept you as you are. I see and know you as my perfect children. Make Love one of your most powerful tools, the one you pick up first for every job that you do. There are many things you do now that you could not do if Love was the tool in your hand.

Which brings me back very satisfactorily to my first question. If Love was the tool in our hand we could not knock each other about, not caring whether we maimed each other!

GROWTH

Dear God, can you describe growth in a way for us to understand? I know we put seeds in a suitable mixture of compost and place them in an appropriate temperature, but that does not cause them to GROW; that cannot give them strength. We place a rose-bud in water and it gradually opens out, but the water isn't actually causing the petals to move surely? A hen sits on her eggs to keep them warm, but that isn't moving the chick inside the shell. At least, that description doesn't satisfy me!

As I have said before, you cannot see Love, but you know it is there. You cannot see Truth, but you know when you hear it. You experience the outward signs, the results of these phenomena, but you cannot see the working, the actual movement. You cannot see air, electricity, sound.

You do not see your soul, but it is there.

Can YOU see these unseen things?

I put them there, I see them 'working'. How do you explain your taste, smell, hearing, sight, touch? You accept that they are there – or sometimes not there.

Recall what I tell you about the Power of Thought, the Power of Prayer. You cannot see Thought and Power. You feel these things. You know these things, but you do not know how or why you know them.

You are born with instinct and conscience, but you cannot explain them. How would you describe them to your questioning five-year-old? You would say you 'just know'.

I say to you, Growth is a power and love you cannot see. I cannot show them to you, except physically as a result. You see the seeds come through the soil, you see the petals opening, you see the child grow, but you cannot see the actual movement of growth.

Can you?

Can your liver see itself? Can your kidneys understand their working? Can you 'see' your Mind working? These things of which we speak are all Truth, all Love, all Knowledge at work – part of the Great Intelligence, which you call me, God.

There is no secret about this, but in your mortal state it is difficult, even impossible, for you to grasp this Power.

Why do you think you pour in 'golden light', Christ Light, to your plants and flowers at times, especially when they are showing signs of wilting? Can you explain what you are doing?

I believe that an unseen force is going from me to them through my fingers. I 'see' gold rays pouring down upon them. Love is moving into them.

You are right, but it is difficult for you to explain to the unenlightened what is happening. They have to accept your word for it – or think you somewhat unbalanced!

Now see that same Light and Power and Love pouring down into those seeds, those eggs, those flowers. I know it works; you know it works.

So the answer to your original question is, Growth is Love personified, manifested, manifesting itself. Joy expressed. Bliss experienced. Thought manifested. Me Manifested.

That is a lovely explanation. Thank you.

16.5.01

It seems weeks since I tuned-in, yet it is little more than a fortnight. I feel quite guilty when I neglect this work.

I have never received a satisfactory explanation as to why we had the Great Gale of October 1987. It swept across England in a wide band, causing dreadful damage to trees and landscapes, yet hardly killing anyone. Countless stories were told of how a tree had just missed a house or a church; in some cases a vehicle was stopped by a tree in front, then one went down just behind, trapping the driver, yet doing him no harm.

Was there a reason for that gale and was it some kind of lesson for us which we may not have learned?

You are recalling how it happened during the night, when comparatively few people were about, little traffic on your roads. This was an unusual occurrence on your little island. In other parts of the world hurricanes, tornadoes, earth quakes, volcanic eruptions are more frequent.

You, here, were not prepared. In other countries there is often warning, warning signs, preparations made, preparation made from past experiences.

These mighty happenings show man how powerful storms are. Man can see how puny he is compared with real Power, how he has no control over these mighty forces. You can learn (and remember) from these happenings the meaning of POWER.

You have a saying, "Get back in your pram". Well these happenings cause man to realise how powerless he is on his own, of his own volition. It causes a lot of thought. It 'puts down the mighty'.

Sometimes man learns to pray in these circumstances, because he doesn't know what else to do. When you are really frightened, terrified, distraught, you turn to Me, often as a last resort.

Did Angels direct that gale here? It seems to my little mind that there were mighty, loving souls, guiding those blasts between buildings, making them avoid harming human beings, as if we were divinely protected during that night?

A friend asked you recently if you think people work in heaven and you told her you believe you choose to do what you wish.

Now there are as many jobs on your next plane as you are used to here on earth. There are many more jobs and they are much easier to come by. You do not need a CV or a character reference – nor a salary! You choose what appeals to you most. There are those who choose to comfort the bereaved or the dying; those who choose to guide your botanists and horticulturists; those who choose to protect you from harm, to mention just a few.

Now you see, on that night in question, these latter souls chose to protect their brothers (and sisters) on the earth plane. So that while you learned a great lesson in the Power of what you call Nature, there were those who chose to protect you in the process.

You, yourself, feel you are able to ask the angels to part the clouds for sunshine at certain times. You picture a mightiness pushing the clouds away to let through the sunshine. And when it happens you feel it cannot be so! Yet you learned in your White Eagle work how the ancient tribes called down a blessing on their crops. They used their soul-power to call down love, growth; it was their 'fertiliser' and the same can be done now. No artificial fertilisers, no poisons that kill off necessary bacteria and insects – just love and faith.

Much of this is done, but man is afraid of being ridiculed, as you yourself are, so it is not talked about.

You call down divine protection on people, places, plants, buildings. We talked about this before – how you can protect others, and yourselves, against accident, against abuse.

There are lessons to be absorbed from Great Power, and from your own, what you would call, little Power. All is from Me, or what you can call the Great Intelligence.

Sometimes you do not ask for help or a sign, but you, yourself, remember those signs on a certain day in your life when you were given what you knew to be a special blessing – proof of approval or, in other words, an approval to you and your beloved.

There is so much joy, undreamed of joy, awaiting you all, my children. Look out for it now, you do not have to wait until you are on this side.

Bless you all.

KILLING

23.5.01

How I enjoyed that gardening yesterday – working for nearly ten hours, with only two short breaks. I am so grateful for my energy. Working with plants at this time of year makes me so aware of growth and how miraculous it is. What bothers me slightly – no quite a lot – is my treatment of the wild life. A robin spends much time so close to me I have to be careful not to hit him by mistake, and I send him great love as I watch him. Then I bless the bees doing their important job with the pollen, and I am careful not to destroy the centipedes and worms. However, I kill slugs, snails and leather-jackets. I just say 'Sorry chum, you are not wanted here', and I have sprayed insecticide on the blight on the lupins.

Now I feel you are going to remind me that we should not kill anything. I find this hard to accept when I see those little monsters ruining the plants. And what about midges that nearly drive us crazy, especially in parts of Scotland. Where do we stand here?

You are picturing a bright green caterpillar eating away at your beautiful pink rose bud as it lies across the grey velvet.

You have written a book called 'Time Was My Enemy', and that is the cause of much suffering – Time. In a perfect world you would collect up the caterpillars and put them on a hedge for the birds to feed on, as with other insects. When you have all learned not to harm the small birds and mammals they will come close enough to be working with you at all times. There will be no fear and it is natural for there to be predators.

When more birds are again prevalent there will be less blight too, even midges will be less troublesome. Wasps do important work and will not harm you if you do not annoy them and give out bad vibrations.

Everyone on your part of the planet is in such a hurry; you have not time to let nature take its course.

Man was once a predator, but he has learned, or is learning, not to be so cruel as he used to be. Vegetarianism is growing daily, sometimes coming about by the revolting pictures you see on your television screens. There is a slow movement towards becoming more humane and thus more healthy in your bodies and your minds.

This brings us to the pictures of the fighting and stone-throwing in the East. Can any of you see any good being done by this? Is any result occurring for the Peace of the earth?

Women and children are living in terror. When you say your prayers for peace, divide the mothers and children from the men. Different rays are required for each. See violence being destroyed by the ray of Peace, and comfort and strength being given by the ray of Love and moral strength.

Women are endeavouring to become equal with men, but you do not feel them wanting to be warlike, vicious, cruel. Pray that women may reign, as was so, many, many thousands of years ago.

This is why I keep saying pray, pray, pray. I tell you Thought is so strong and prayer so powerful it will be the means of the beginning of a lasting peace on earth, for which you all long.

Who is listening to this wise counselling? How can it reach where it is needed?

You know the reading matter which keeps coming your way and how anxious you are for more. Picture that multiplied by thousands per day, yes per day. It may seem a slow process to you, but it is spreading, unseen, but not unnoticed.

In your own small environment you are feeling this brotherly love from those who were strangers to you less than two years ago. You can all create harmony and give out love and that joins with other harmony and love. Remember No Space, No Time. A few droplets soon become a puddle; a puddle soon becomes a lake; a lake can overflow and become a flood. So is it with love and your longing, all of you, for peace and harmony.

Politics and religion are supposed to be taboo subjects in general conversation. It seems to me now that it is so important that we get the right people to govern our country. I don't care what 'party' it is so long as they are strong, honest and truly have the best interests of our country and the world at heart. Does it help for us to pray for the caring people to rule us?

If you all were able to vote for the most worthy and effective member of your community to represent you there would be no 'party politics'. Liken this idea to children at a party or teachers in a school; those with leadership powers and who organise with fairness and love become role models. There is nothing wrong with idealism put into practice. Leaders need to be completely unselfish (rather a rare attribute), far sighted, understanding and fair in all considerations. Strong for the weak, understanding for the poor, but wise for the rebellious. There would be less legislation because no underhandedness would be tolerated in a fair and honest State.

111

As with the first country to give up armaments that we talked about the other day, who is brave enough to start a completely new, yet obviously simple and just, way of government?

You all have much food for thought.

What a wonderful conversation. It started off with insects and finished up with affairs of State! Thank you.

FORGIVENESS

I know you have talked about Forgiveness in other books, but will you please say more about it here, with all its implications?

Forgive, forgive, forgive, for you know not what causes others to behave as they do. If they could see from your viewpoint they would not behave as they do. If you had not reached the point at which you are now you would not behave as you do.

A young child cries for what it wants, has tantrums, screams, because it has not learned discipline or how else to get its own way. It does not know there is usually a better way to behave. With time it learns; it has to be encouraged to give as well as take, to think of others, not always to please itself.

So with adults, sometimes they listen to false messages within themselves and they act, often on impulse, without sufficient thought – either for themselves or for others.

To forgive what you think you see as wrong in others, or a wrong act, is to cleanse yourself. In other words, do not judge.

Trying to become perfect is not easy; you travel a stony path, you have to look where you are going at all times. You can help lead another along that path and still look where you are going, but when you follow another already on the path, you are often surprised at the route they take. You have not seen something ahead that they may have seen.

Trust those who set a good example, follow those who know the way. Sometimes you have to leave others behind for they are not ready to tread that difficult route. They need to remain on the easier route.

You see this is all to do with becoming evolved. The Highly Evolved Beings you have read about can see ahead, they can look on. Do not expect others to follow your path; they may not be ready. Sometimes they have to stumble and learn by their mistakes. You learn more by making mistakes than by following exactly what you read in some instructions.

But surely it is better to read the instructions first, then try to carry out what they explain?

Read and try to learn at all times, but if you never do the practical things yourself how do you know you have taken in what you have read?

When you forgive someone you are putting into practice what you have read. You have learned the lesson of for-giving, pre-giving, them.

When you are unforgiving you are not being an example of Good. Forgive those that trespass against you. Have you not trespassed against others during your life?

Ignorance is bliss, but ignorance and bliss do not get you anywhere, except for a nice feeling at that moment. Knowledge and forgiveness do get you somewhere. And do you know where? You feel nearer to me, nearer to the Source of your Being.

How do we forgive those who ill-treat children?

They are inflicting their vengeance on a helpless child. They have an inner rage. They experience a feeling of 'winning' because their victim is helpless.

Then would they not learn from being victimised themselves; from experiencing terror, pain? You are going to say two wrongs do not make a right, I can feel it coming!

Yes, because by inflicting pain on them you are adding fuel to fire. You are making that person more inhuman. The criminal is more likely to learn from pictures of the result of his crimes, than from experiencing them, for even as he inflicts that pain he is obtaining what he thinks is power and satisfaction.

It takes a long time to teach a wild animal to be tame; it is filled with fear, mistrust, yet see that same wild animal with its young and you are amazed at its gentleness, its instinct of love, patience, care. You could not teach that animal to be a good parent by thrashing it.

But all this doesn't help the victim. How about the damage that has been done to that child, or terrified person?

Sometimes those souls have chosen to be an example. Sometimes they have chosen to bring out compassion in other mortals, as I told you before when talking about the sick and homeless and starving in other countries. As to the harm done to young children, you do not know why they chose for that to happen to them, yes chose. Their lives may appear to have been blighted in their present lifetime, but their rewards are great in higher realms. Those are the wonders that await you to be learned when you evolve, or return to your higher self.

You are never alone. You know that.

PAIN

Tell me about terrific pain. How do some people bear great pain and how are others able to cope with looking on?

This also is like the lesson on forgiveness. The one in pain and the onlooker find their great inner strength, their stamina and their compassion, their faith and belief. You are never given more than you can bear, remember?

When we do not have to bear those things in a lifetime, does it mean that we have already coped with it in another life or that we will have to cope with it in a future life?

You forget that you have lived so many lives; you have experienced so much that you do not remember. Sometimes people think that they are re-living something – and they are, because so much of what happens during your present life-span has happened before. Each time the same lesson can teach a different aspect. Each situation has so many facets. There are so many kinds of love and so many kinds of pain; so many acts of kindness and so many acts of understanding. What you do not experience you cannot understand. If you had never felt pain or seen a sunset how would you explain them to another? How would you learn compassion if you had not suffered? How would you learn tolerance if you had never had to tolerate anything?

I have talked about these things at length in CWG. You cannot experience one experience without having experienced the opposite!

CHILDLESSNESS

Are some couples meant NOT to have children so that they know what it is like to want them and not have them? Therefore, is it right to interfere with 'nature' in those cases by medical means?

No soul comes to this earth plane by mistake. You all chose to come here and to whom and by what means. It is true that ways have been found to inseminate the female species artificially, that is what you think of as progress, but it is not to say that it is right or wrong. I have told you, you have free choice. But it does not mean that you should not be learning from your actions. Look what you have been causing to your earth itself, to its structure, and to your plants, their taste, their resistance, their balance. Mostly you keep away from wasps' nests, but sometimes you get many nasty stings. Usually that teaches you a lesson, painfully too.

LEARNING FROM EXPERIENCE

Do you sometimes despair of us?

Where would that leave you? You are already like ships without rudders, you would then be like ships without a captain.

You must already know the outcome of all our actions.

Yes, all is now. Nothing is new. You forget to remember! So much you have experienced before, but you do not remember the consequences so you have to re-learn to put right your mistakes.

Is it tedious for you?

It is interesting and sometimes it is amazing how long it takes you to learn. When you watch a baby trying to walk or a spider spinning a web or a bird making a nest or a beginner learning to become a tailor, all that is as nothing compared with watching my children learning to live harmoniously.

I should think HEBs must laugh at us and our antics.

You could say they are amused, but not in the way of laughing AT you or criticising you or judging you. They are just sorry that you do not learn quicker.

I suppose we have never been HEBs or we would not chose to return to this un-evolved plane?

While on the earth plane you do not choose to return to being a helpless baby; likewise you do not return once you have become much evolved. Yes, I know you are thinking of those who become senile while on this earth, but that is a different scenario.

Why do some of us become senile?

Because you still believe in death and deterioration.

You shed your outer coat, but you do not change your Being. You proceed to another place, but you do not die. You are born with all knowledge, but you do not choose to use it enough, therefore you absorb a lot of false information. You get led astray by those who think they know more than they do. You listen to false prophets. You believe too much of what you hear or read instead of picking out the Truths. You know all Truth in your innermost. You, yourself, know that. You have to sort it over carefully. Sometimes you can pass it on, sometimes it is better to keep quiet. It is waste to throw pearls before swine.

That makes me ask about Foot & Mouth Disease that has been so severe on this island recently. I feel we have dealt with it badly – not in the right way, possibly causing more trouble?

Your old enemy FEAR set in; Fear and Panic. Fear spread like a forest fire from farm to farm, from veterinary surgeon to veterinary surgeon, from person to person. Fear of contagion, fear for livelihoods, fear of loss of control. Then fear spread to towns and villages that provide holiday accommodation. Having killed thousands of animals there was panic as to what to do with their remains, then fear of what the burying of them is causing. Oh, dear, what a terrible dose of fear and panic.

I don't think that is going to look very helpful in print and coming from YOU!

No, but it is the Truth and the truth often hurts. When you have an outbreak of measles or tuberculosis you do not kill off everybody who has been within a mile of that outbreak; you separate the sick from the well and you treat the sick in the best way you know how. Your doctors and nurses do feel fear, but they do not panic. And what else happens? Thousands of you PRAY for the sick. And remember the power of prayer? Animals need prayer just as people and nations do. Circles of Light can be placed around the sick and the well, the contagious and the healthy, and the farmers and the vets and the B&Bs can all be held in that great Light that so many of you know about.

Surely there must have been a lot of prayer during this time?

If you put a pound of flour on one side of the scales and a few feathers on the other, which will weigh the most? I did not say a pound of feathers, I said a few feathers.

LIFE AFTER DEATH (II)

When we pass over – I refuse to say die – how aware are we of what is going on back here on the earth plane?

When picturing your pink rose bud, you saw it tucking a hand, so to speak, under its head and having a sleep! Those who have suffered long before letting go, arrive, in what you think of as heaven, very tired. All they want is to rest and sleep in peace. This they do to recover from their seemingly long journey. Others arrive awake, joyful, and rearing to get on with their new life, as you, yourself, anticipate doing.

According to how much you have absorbed or remembered while on earth, so your thoughts put you in the situations that you picture. You are with those you wish to be with, you know that thought will bring everything to you, both situations and people. Remember, you are returning to familiar territory. Liken it to returning to a place where you have spent a wonderful holiday and you are full of joy at revisiting all your old haunts. Your joy in meeting those you love is indescribable.

You relish your re-found feeling of complete wellness, no pain, no disabilities, no limitations as to your movements. Your thoughts are giving you instantaneous results.

How soon can we look back, or down, to earth to see what is going on and how those are coping that we have left behind?

That depends on your innermost wishes and the strength of your soul-being. You will be surrounded by loving beings, both known and unknown (seemingly) to you. They will know what is best for you and how much you can withstand. No loving Being wishes you to experience spiritual indigestion. You do not give an invalid very rich food, you nurse them back to health gradually, just as here when you arrive full of power and

117

strength you can withstand so much more. You are prepared for so much more; you have done your homework back on earth. All is gentleness.

Does it upset us to see our loved ones suffering because of our passing?

That depends on your strength, as I have just explained. You long to let them know you are alive and so happy, you long to embrace them and comfort them. Sometimes you do this through other means.

Do you mean through mediums?

Yes. A good medium can contact them with comforting words. If they are really seeking communication they sometimes feel drawn to a spiritual meeting or a spiritual person. You ask for safe contact both for yourself and for them. Sometimes this is the beginning of another soul believing in life after death.

Many souls still on earth are so afraid of what they consider the occult, or spiritualism or the unknown. It is right for them to be careful and wary, but if all is done in prayer and love no harm is caused and much comfort received.

Is it frustrating for the newly arrived soul not to be able to contact those left behind?

You do not experience frustration; you can know disappointment, but there are always those who will explain to you how best to 'behave', for the sake of a better word. It is so much easier to receive instant help in your new state. Whereas on earth you contact a solicitor, a doctor, a priest, a healer, literature, which all takes so long, here you can gain instantly all knowledge and help.

You have explained in other books what happens when a non-believer finds himself or herself 'not dead'. Are those people frightened?

Surprised, amazed, astonished are better words of explanation. It can be what you would call a slow process, but there is no time so it matters not. You would be surprised at how many people make a last-minute switch from being a non-believer to believing, very near the end of their lives. They make what you might call a death-wish that they are going on to another life instead of nothingness. Oh, dear ones, only believe what I keep telling you – there is NO DEATH.

That brings me to asking about the death of Jesus. I believed his soul left his body while on the cross and went straight to heaven. Now I have watched a Sai Baba video and that has given me a whole new train of thought. It would account for his body having disappeared. Is it true that when Joseph of Arimathea took his body, wonderful healing herbs were used and Jesus recovered, then lived on for many years, partly in India?

Was there anything to stop him from choosing to use his same body to go on living on earth? His 'coat' was repaired instead of discarded. So much love was with him from so many souls both on earth and in heaven. His faith was so great that he could work miracles. He was one of the Great Masters for whom nothing was impossible. He chose to go on living.

Where can I read and learn more about this 'story'?

Chose for the right knowledge to come to you. The right books will come to you from unexpected quarters. You are learning to choose instead of to want or need. You are learning that it works. Go on with your choosing and your belief and your work. I have told you we do not waste our resources.

Put your spiritual power to more use. Choose to meet up with others of like mind. Choose to progress and you will. Bless you my child.

Thank you dear God. May I be worthy of this teaching and the comfort that it brings me and the friends who come to me with love, and the situations that change according to my trying to think the right way. Thank you.

EGO

Will you tell us more about our ego and what it does to us.

Your ego is the little mind that thinks it knows all the answers! It has its uses, giving you self-confidence and a feeling of 'boosting your morale' as you sometimes say. It helps you to achieve your goals; it makes you feel 'good'.

When you let it rule your life you become hard to tolerate. You can use your ego to make your thoughts and circumstances agree with everything you do and say. In other words, you can appear very self-righteous.

The real you, your Higher Mind, seeks for higher Truth. The ego prevents you from feeling humility – or it can make you think you are being humble.

119

When you remember that you are all equal and all have the inner power and knowledge to raise your thoughts to knowledge outside yourself, to communicate with the Higher Intelligence, you suppress your ego and listen with more knowledge and accuracy.

Become still and know Me, your higher self. Let your lower mind pass through your head, but stop to listen to your inner knowledge. All answers, all knowledge, are yours. The rose opens as it develops, you cannot improve on its growth.

How do we equate this with the writings of Louise Hay, where she tells us so frequently to "approve of yourself"?

When she writes in that vein she is encouraging you to love yourself, to see the real you, the perfect you. She is telling you to rise above your lower self that keeps pulling you down and taking away your self-esteem. There is a great difference in these two circumstances.

Can you give us an analogy please?

You do your French homework and you are afraid you will forget what you have learned, that you will be inadequate for your tests, that you will sound or look foolish in front of others. That is when you need to tell yourself that you have done your best, you have used your ability to learn, you will not look or sound foolish to others because they are in the same situation. You are not being told, or telling yourself, that you are better than all the others, that you can glide along without learning on the way, that you can trample on your peers or classmates. Do you see the difference?

Yes, I think so, I need to read what you have said, but please go on further.

You take a part in a play as an amateur. You are nervous before you go on stage, you are afraid. Your turn comes and you do well and the audience claps and makes a fuss of you – then, your ego puffs you out, you may feel the great I Am. But if you had prayed first, before you went on the stage, and you felt an inner confidence and joy, when the clapping commenced your higher self would be full of gratitude and thankfulness for the help you knew you had received from your Higher You, the part of you that is part of me. Your whole attitude would be different. Does that help you?

Yes, definitely. That makes a clear difference between our ego and our real self, the You-Self.

I like that expression of me. The Me-Self.

Does the ego hold a lot of us back from progressing?

It can delay your real progress. Fear comes into this explanation of the ego. The ego is afraid to let go in case it loses its power, whereas by letting go the real you gains power, undreamed of power and love. It is the old conflict between fear and love. The one knows mainly fear, the other knows no fear.

I was diffident about asking this question and of not getting the answer right.

Yes, I know you were. You still doubt yourself – and Me!

I am sorry. Perhaps it is MY ego!

I forgive you, just forgive yourself.

ILLNESS

Does certain food really upset us or is it all in our minds?

You are talking about the little mind?

Yes, of course.

The little mind loves to take control, to tell you what is right and what it thinks is wrong, what it wishes you to believe and what it wishes you to discard as false. You get what you call 'a bee in your bonnet' and when certain foods are put before you, or even talked about, the bee buzzes around and says that will harm you or upset you. You listen to it; you believe it and so those foods do upset you. Your Higher Mind knows nothing can harm its perfect manifestation. It declares all is well at all times.

But what about babies and young children who really are allergic to milk or wheat or some other product, and how about people who have migraines when they eat cheese or chocolate?

There was an origin for that thought. A seed of doubt or fear was sown in that little mind and where children are concerned it was the parent who took on board the belief that their child was caused to become ill by certain foods, probably a seed sown by a medic or a 'family history'. This is another case of fear manifesting.

121

But I know of people, sensible people, who have children or grandchildren who cannot take certain foods without becoming really ill.

You are believing what those parents are telling you. You are adding weight to their beliefs.

But I couldn't say 'it is all in your mind, just feed the child normally'. It would be most presumptuous of me.

Yes, it would from the standpoint of your little mind. Suppose you used your Higher Mind, which knows all Truth, and said with conviction 'No harm can come to anyone by eating wholesome, untreated, natural food. It is the chemicals, the sprays, the preservatives, the colours, the additives, that are the real cause of the seeming trouble.'

But I have no authority to say something like that.

I have just explained your authority – Higher Mind versus Little Mind.

Do you mean nothing in the way of food can harm anyone? I wouldn't feed an invalid on steak and kidney pie or a baby on lobster.

I hope you would not feed ANYONE on steak, kidney or lobster. That is part of your digestive troubles. Do not kill your brother animals and eat them. Do not spray your crops with pesticides, do not pollute your waters with diesel oil and chemicals.

You are saying that, when we return to pure food, we shall all be much healthier?

I am saying you will all be healthy.

I suppose this all comes back to our money problem. Scientists, so-called food experts, great pharmaceutical companies are not going to want to stop their tampering and their profit-making. They brainwash us.

You have made your lives so complicated. Eat wholesome food, unadulterated food, home prepared food. As with the treatment of garden grubs and the birds we talked about earlier, you can return to more simple ways of living and it will be less costly. But Time is your enemy. Remember?

People just don't want to spend time preparing food and cooking it. I have watched programmes on television about this. They get no pleasure from domestic jobs, which they call chores.

122

You have forgotten how to live as a tribe! You think that sounds primitive. I tell you, what you do and how you live now is very primitive. You get further and further away from simplicity, unselfishness, giving, helping, loving one another. All is speed – and for what? Where is everyone heading? Re-read "The Last Hours of Ancient Sunlight" and "The Prophet's Way" by Thom Hartmann. You can all learn much from those writings. But some of you do not want to learn.

How about aches and pains and skin conditions – are they all connected with our thinking?

Do you think your back can say 'I am going to have a bad pain' or that your skin says 'I am going to itch like hell' just to prove I have a mind of my own?' You believe in ageing and you see the result. You believe that your hair can turn grey or white just because you are ageing, you believe your bones wear out just because you are ageing. Who says so? You do. You have believed this for centuries.

There is the story of the 21 year-old woman who believed she was always 21 and when she 'died' in old age, she still looked 21 – because she had believed it. We are back to the power of thought.

Your body obeys you. Expect trouble and usually it comes. Expect poverty and you experience it. Expect that getting wet will cause you a pain in your shoulders and you will most likely feel it.

Clean out your minds. Throw out all the useless thoughts that fill up valuable space. Examine each item and if it is of no use, throw it out. Then add all the real items for a healthy life. Decide to stock only pure, natural foods, exercise all your components, oil the locks, tighten the muscles with exercise, straighten the curved bones, caused through bad posture.

Now throw out more negative thoughts, all criticism and judgment; stop believing that anything, yes anything, can harm you. Know that you are in that beam of pure light that gives you only good. Feel it, breathe it, relax in it. You have free choice in all things – use it, all the time.

Now decide to meditate at least once a day, when you will know the Truth, you will think kindly and lovingly of others, you will send this Light to others and to all the world. Do all this with love, unconditional love. Be kind to all those you meet. If you cannot afford to give to a beggar, stop and talk to him, give him hope and a smile and explain you cannot give him cash. Do not be so afraid of admitting who you are. Then remember how rich you are compared with him or her. Maybe then you will turn back and give him a coin.

All that you give with love comes back to you in some form of good, be it friendship or help or thoughtfulness. Count your blessings. Make a list of them. Cross off your grouses because there are so many so much worse off than you. Give of your good thoughts and send out your blessings, which are my blessings, at all times. Do these things daily and in one week you will see how your life has changed – and perhaps how you have changed the life of another.

All this is lovely teaching, but how does it apply to the blind, the terminally ill, those with eczema, those with broken bones?

When you include those in your prayers that is how they can be helped; their spirit lifts, they experience hope. You are given the chance to talk to them, to let them hear you say how good your next life will be, how much there is to look forward to. How temporary this life is.

I think many of them would tell me where to go with my ideas!

If only one is helped it will have been worth taking the knocks and ridicule from the others.

But how do I help my special friend with her itchy skin that nothing seems to cure? She is lapping up all this teaching and really takes in all I read to her, for she is also partially sighted. I feel so useless in this case.

She knows how to help herself. Let her continue to use her own method until she receives an answer. This is not satisfying you, yourself. Trust me and trust your son to me. Continue to hold them in the Light. That is YOUR work for them.

WHAT GOOD IS PRAYER?

15.7.01

Dear God,

I thought the delay in my continuing this conversation with you was because I had run out of questions. Those that came to me I realised you had dealt with in CWG.

Now I think my lack of enthusiasm is because I am disappointed, disheartened, disillusioned, dismayed and disgusted as I watch the state of the world in general. We seem to be going backwards instead of forwards.

124

In most countries there is unrest, if not outright fighting. I cannot see a lessening of the starvation in the East, the homelessness and cruelty in the middle East, the greed in Europe and America, the continued fighting and hatred in Northern Ireland and now the rioting and racism in our own large cities.

What good is prayer doing? Who is listening? Who really wants conditions to improve? Men, yes literally men, not women, seem to enjoy fighting, injuring and killing each other. Peace talks concerning Ireland, and Israel and Palestine seem a waste of time.

You have said how surprised we would be if we could see the amount of good our prayers do. I wish I could see an example of this good happening.

Few seem satisfied with their lot. Is it greed and jealousy at work? Amongst my own friends and acquaintances I don't see them wanting a bit of their neighbour's land or a bigger car like their neighbours have or an equal opportunity in being able to do the same as other people. Oh, how thankful I am to be happy with my material lot. There are so many worse off than I am – and those who are better off do not seem happier, in fact they are often dissatisfied and only wanting more and more.

Even local rules become senseless. There are some old, dilapidated buildings about with no particular beauty and a council slaps a label on them calling them 'listed'. Why? Some stand as blots on the landscape. Now I have just discovered that budding florists have to learn rules about what should and should not go in flower arrangements, labelling them if they contain anything considered poisonous! We were taught not to eat certain berries and fruits and not to suck certain weed stems when we were small. Have parents lost all sense of responsibility now? Perhaps soon our hedgerows will have to bear notices saying 'do not eat any of this'.

Oh, how cynical and frustrated I feel at times. New rules and regulations are now made in Europe that have to apply to all countries belonging to the EU. Is this good? Can we not decide for ourselves, as countries, what is best for us. Anyway, the USA isn't trying to cut down fuel emissions into the atmosphere, Russia doesn't want to stop making weapons of destruction. Most countries seem guilty of exporting materials that eventually go to making ammunition in another country. Where is it all going to end?

We are so far from being 'all one' with love for each other. I think you indicated earlier on that it would be better if we all stayed in the country in which we were born. Was Enoch Powell right when he advised against immigrants all those years ago?

How can we put right all the things we have done wrong? Are you going to say there is no right and wrong? I suppose if I had a young family and was homeless in London I would resent accommodation being given to a refugee who had just arrived. But I must say I would not expect to go to, say, Jerusalem and be given a house before a local Jew.

And while I am having a grouse, how can we be so crazy as to let clubs pay millions of pounds to 'buy' a man to kick a ball about when that money could go towards building Homes to house the helpless elderly who are taking up hospital beds wanted for those who need nursing?

And why do young people scream and clamour to watch others (who have never been trained to sing properly) just screech and make ugly faces and antics? Where has the beauty of dance and song gone?

And why isn't the Lottery money limited to a top prize of, say, œ5 million, with the balance going towards health and teaching?

Surely these thoughts and questions aren't the produce of old age, but of deep, educated thinking?

Do you feel better for 'getting all that off your chest'?

No, not really. I feel somewhat ashamed that I haven't remembered better all that you have been teaching me these last months. I have 'forgotten to remember'.

15.9.01

What a terrible catastrophe has happened in America. The 11th of this month has affected the whole world. We in other countries have been mentally and physically affected by this disaster; how ever must those be feeling who are right near the demolished buildings and those who have lost dear ones? We can only try to feel their grief.

Please tell us how best to help these devastated souls and how best to avoid a Third World War. It must be difficult for revenge not to be felt, yet it could be catastrophic.

Pray for those suffering souls who are left on the earth plane; pray for them to be comforted by their guardian angels, their guides and their teachers. Pray that they may be open to receive comfort and pray that they may become aware that those whom they think met such a terrible death were immediately on a higher plane. Their 'death' was so quick they did not have what you call 'time' to be frightened, to feel great pain. Their passing over was instantaneous.

This knowledge will comfort and sustain their dear ones left behind. Pray that they may talk to me, knowing that I will comfort them.

Now also pray for the perpetrators who caused all this suffering. They need your prayers also. Hold them also in the Light and pray that they too may feel their guardian angels and guides near them. They have gained nothing by their actions. If you go to their countries and devastate their people, how will you be 'better' than they are? Two wrongs do not make a right and anyway, I keep telling you there is no wrong nor right. There is only the way of Love – Love without Fear.

Hold all world leaders in the Light of Love that they may be sensitive to right guidance. So much Fear is being generated and it spreads like a contagious disease. Remember Love is much stronger and that too can spread like a beautiful cloak over all the world. Prayer and Love are so powerful. Put them to the test. Listen in your hearts for I am speaking to all of you at all times. Listen for Good thoughts and trust me at all times.

Great wings of Love and Comfort envelope you and all who suffer.

Every time you think about all that has been happening, the consequences, the perpetrators, try very hard to push out all negative thoughts and thoughts of fear. Replace your thoughts every time with Love and Trust. Use the Light over ALL. A great lesson can be learned through this disaster.

Open wide your arms and your hearts, send forth the Light, knowing that it reaches all those to whom you send it, be they what you call good or evil. Remember always that Love overcomes all; it is a mighty force and can save your world.

It is not easy for you to push away fear, especially at this time, but you CAN DO IT, Keep replacing it with Love and Trust.

I never leave you – use Me.

God bless you my children – I am your loving father and I know only Good for you all. Do not dwell on the horror. There is no death – just different dimensions. Help little children to understand these Truths; explain to them in your own ways how they can help and how they can be comforted.

It is so important that you do not want revenge. What will it solve to make thousands of my children suffer in a like fashion, whatever their ages and nationalities and religions?

Come to me in the silence of your innermost and I will comfort you. The Light of Good has been mighty as you have held your Services and Silences during the last few days. Keep it up. Pray. I love you all. I never leave you. Bless you.

SUFFERING IN ILLNESS

Why do people have to suffer in illness for so long, even when they are basically 'good' people?

Firstly, there are no 'bad' people. You are all my perfect creation, Good, perfect, part of Me.

I have told you before, it is you who try to make my children good or bad by your judgments, your criticisms, your trying to create icons or demons. If you go outside and have a tantrum others will look on and make judgments – thinking either you are in a temper or distraught or unbalanced. Mostly others looking on will take no notice or at best try to calm you down, or perhaps join you. No one will have been altered basically and all will settle down. If on the other hand you are a well-known personality, word will go round fast as to how you were perceived to behave, it will become newsworthy, printed in your newspapers in large

128

print, a news item on your television screens. You can give power to others, you can take power from others and you can give away your own power. Think about that.

How has this happened? Because you are making judgments, some of you thrive on gossip or scandal. A mountain has been created out of a mole hill.

So, you are all good people. As to suffering in illness for whatever length of 'time', you, the onlooker, do not know what that soul is learning or remembering. You all need to "wake up" and sometimes those who suffer most wake up sooner. When you wake up from your illusions, you realise what a lot you have remembered about Who You Really Are. Most of you still have to remember there is no time, for in all eternity how can there be time?

Those of you who look on at suffering are also learning and remembering. My Love is with each one of you at all times. By looking on with Love and not Fear you are helping your brother/sister to become strong. You are handing over to them your compassion. You see only the centre of the book, not what you would call the beginning and the end, in other words the complete story.

You expect the heaven world to be perfect. Why? Because you see only Love in action. When will you put Love into action on your earth plane?

Hand over those you love to Me and I will comfort not only them, but you also. I will be sharing your load, which was given to you to enable you to progress. It is true that you are never given more than you can bear.

THE POWER OF PRAYER

Do we do more harm than good when we pray hard for people to live or be healed, when it is their karma to suffer or die?

There is no death, NO DEATH. When you leave Manchester and go to Buxton, you have not died en route; when you return to Manchester you have not died in Buxton, but you have returned home. Karma is a form of recompense, both painful and enjoyable. What you sow, so shall you reap. When you are being kind or unkind you are affecting yourself just as much as the other soul. You need to forgive yourself for there is really no point in forgiving another. You were judging them in the first place.

129

Pray for others to 'wake up', pray for them to accept there is a great strength around them to weave into. You all chose to return to this earth plane, when you did and with whom, and for a purpose, which you have forgotten. You do not know, you cannot see, what others are here to remember, although as you progress it becomes clearer to you how life unfolds. You cannot do harm with prayer, but you can do seeming harm with wrong thinking. Pray for all your world to have Peace, for all your leaders, in all countries, to be open to Guidance for Peace, and for those you love to be comforted, strengthened and held in my Love. For whether any of these prayers are believed or felt, you are causing a channel for my Love and Light to guide and reach these conditions.

You cause your own suffering – man's inhumanity to man.

You could pray for a nest of ants or a hive of bees or a group of monks – all their needs would be different, but they all deserve their space and their life, their guidance, their work; they all need Light and Love and I know how to help them, Trust Me.

GUARDIAN ANGELS

Do we all have Guardian Angels, do we keep the same ones, and is it possible for more than one person to share the same Guardian Angel?

When you chose to re-incarnate you chose who your parents would be; you did not make that decision alone, you sought guidance and another soul chose to spend that incarnation with you as your friend and guide, but not in an earth body. Once you were born your parents, or at least your mother, were with you in most cases. As you grew up in earth years others took over some of your care in the form of teachers, tutors, real, true friends, but your parents were usually in the background, there if you wanted them.

Sometimes you have thought you were alone because no humans seemed to be around when you needed them. But I tell you, you are never alone. Your Guide is always there, joined by now with others who are watching your development and interested in your progress.

Now you can tune-in to several 'friends' on a higher plane. There is no Space. You not only forget there is no Space, but you forget we are all ONE. I am in you and you are in Me and I am that Guide or that Angel, there is no separation. When you tune-in to them you are tuning in to Me.

When your parents pass on they do not leave you and they choose to watch your progress. You are choosing to watch your children's or your siblings' progress. A great bond exists and you begin to realise the Oneness of Life. You can love many people, you can choose to follow many people, to learn with and about many people. When you 'come back home' to a higher plane you can choose to be and to do what benefits you and those with whom you wish to be with in close contact.

Look at the book you are reading – it is on a table, there is no space between it and the table; the table is on the floor, there is no space between the table and the floor. If you upset a glass of water, the glass falls to the floor, whether whole or broken, but it lands somewhere. And the water has run down or across to something. Ah, your scientists will say, "It may have evaporated, changed its substance"! Yes, but it is still there in some form. It cannot not be. You cannot not be.

You are never alone. You never die. You are never forgotten. You are never lost. Whether you are conscious of one or five guides and guardian angels, it makes no difference to what IS. You can contact others with your Higher Mind; you can always contact Me. It is a matter of inner knowing and a desire to do so. No one is outside my Being. Use Me.

DIVINE INTERVENTION

Please God can you help us to understand why there appears to be no divine intervention to prevent innocent children from being abused?

The simple answer is because I have given you free will. You choose to act as you do, to abuse, to fight, to kill, to annihilate, to judge, to dictate, to fear, to be right – instead of just To Be. Your other choice is kindness, peace, thoughtfulness, understanding, brotherly love.

When you choose these latter things, there will be no more wars, no more armaments, no more fear, no more starvation. Thousands upon thousands of you are praying now for this to happen. I have spoken elsewhere about this, many times. Make a Reality of your Oneness, choose for Peace to reign over all your world, between all countries, all your religions. Each one of you by prayer, sincere prayer, unselfish prayer, can add so much POWER for Peace to reign.

Greed and Fear are rife – fear of not having enough and greed to hold on to all you have and all you think you want. The more you give the more you will have, and not only you, but all others who are now starving, without food, warmth or clothing. Give, give, give instead of take, take, take.

Think of a perfect flower with many petals – it does not need more, but removing some would ruin its beauty. Your world is that perfect flower.

SEEING INTO THE FUTURE

Do some people really have the gift to see into our future or past lives?

I find it difficult to ask You this question because I know the answer is 'Yes'. I know Life is eternal, without beginning or end; I know there is no space and I am trying to grapple with there being no time. The Fire of London and the Great Plague were over three hundred years ago, they were not now. And we are not entertaining extra terrestrial beings yet, though I think we will in the future. Where is the past and when is the future?

You are in a 'right old muddle here' aren't you? You are trying to work out an analogy to help you, and you can apply it to what you call the past, but when it comes to the future you query free choice. Let Me take over; quieten your busy mind. Picture the dove grey velvet, making your mind a blank.

You know I will answer this question, but you are also doubting.

You do all experience earthly 'time' because you are not advanced enough to understand 'no time'. You, yourself, know that when you reach higher planes Thought will manifest instantaneously.

In CWG ("Conversations with God") Book 3, I explained to Neale how to reverse the order of your thinking from thought, (working out the details), doing the work (making an object) to reality (holding the finished article in your hand). In other words, make a reality of the finished article, then watch it being made, then think about it. Make Realities, Choices, Goals, then endeavour to reach them.

Remember a Want is not always a Need. And while you want something you will never attain it because it will always be one step ahead. Know that all you need is already yours. If you need to move house, picture the kind of house you would like to live in, then choose the area, then think about how you will get there.

Every word you are typing is recorded into your computer and stays there on record. Every thought you are thinking goes on record and stays on the Akashic Records; this is like making entries in your diary. You have entered where you will go for Christmas; you may have arranged your journey, but you have not yet started that journey. But it is all arranged.

Those souls who choose to make use of their psychic powers, and you all can, are able to pick up these past, present and future records because they already exist. Use these methods wisely. Communication is not always perfect. It depends on the medium and the receiver and the sender or source.

Does this help you to understand? You are moving forward, all the 'time', nothing is stationary. You may alter your plan and go somewhere different or by a different route, this is where your free choice comes in.

You can also ask for guidance as to which is the best way to proceed. You can ignore that guidance, that gut feeling, but it may take longer to obtain your goal.

Thank you dear God. I hope this helps others as it has helped me.

HATRED

I have been asked "Why is there hate?"

Hate is the exact opposite of Love. Hate is a strong emotion that not only spoils the hater but affects the hated.

Apply this to a neighbour. You may be irritated by your neighbour; first there is frustration, then this can turn to a feeling of Hate. Why? Because you are not loving your neighbour as yourself and you are hating yourself for being unloving, though you do not always accept that.

Give out Love. Try to understand that other soul. Couldn't there be a reason why they appear to be behaving so? Could they be crying out for Love and Understanding? Are they not able to feel satisfied with their lot? Are they angry?

This is your opportunity to think deeply about these things. Turn your own irritation into peace and love. Send your neighbour, school mate, parent, relative, loving thoughts. Look for their good, which is there. Look for what makes them feel as they do. Perhaps they are full of fear.

Remember we are all One. What you feel about another, you feel about yourself. Turn the other cheek. It works. Find this out for yourself. This is a local way of finding out the power of Love and Prayer. When you see how it works, then see, understand, how it can work in praying for world peace. All countries and peoples need understanding, never hate, always Love.

Fear is your worst enemy and fear creates hate, insecurity, doubt, a cry for help.

Give of yourself, your real self, to others, not just locally, but over all the world.

God bless you all, my dear children.

AFGHANISTAN

27.10.01

We certainly are as little children. We forget what you tell us to do for Peace, just how to pray. Please remind us again dear God, dear Friend.

You are seeing your rose as a deep pink bud and there is a very bright white light on it, yet this light causes no shadows. Do you know why?

Yes, I know it is all around that rose. There is no point at which it is not, therefore there can be no shadow.

That is right. There are no shadows. When the Light Shines it envelops everything, every thing.

Know that Light is shining over every soul connected with that war in Afghanistan. See it over all your Western forces AND over all your seeming enemies, and especially over all those who are filled with fear and suffering.

You can touch their Souls this way, just as you feel uplifted when your physical sun shines on your gardens, you, your countryside. You feel uplifted. That is what you can do for your brothers and sisters, whether they be Afghans or Pakistanis or Americans or British. You can lift and strengthen their very souls.

See each one of them at peace in the midst of turmoil.

Hold all Leaders and Advisers and Chiefs in the Light of Guidance. It IS working. Know you are using Great Power for what it was meant – to make you feel all One, all loved, all protected.

LET THE LIGHT SHINE. Hold it for as long as you can, many times a day; night and morning; live it, breathe it.

Do this also with Northern Ireland. My children there desire Peace, help them to attain it. Do not let doubt and fear have a place in your thoughts. Rise above it. Hold ALL those people there in this mighty Light. See them rejoicing. See them prospering.

It is so easy to slip back to thoughts of fear and mistrust. Cast out fear and fears. Replace them with Love, brotherly Love. Know that Peace is everywhere NOW. Yes, NOW.

You think that is an unlikely situation, but I tell you, it is true. There is Peace everywhere, just as there is Love everywhere, Sunshine everywhere. Tune in to it and realise its reality. See smiling faces, happy people in Ireland.

Now take your mind back to Afghanistan and see Peace above the turmoil. Picture the starving and homeless being fed and clothed. Make a Reality of it. Keep doing this.

Sometimes mental work can seem harder than physical work, but the result is far greater, more widespread, there are no limits, no boundaries.

I have told you many times, I love all my children equally, whether they are behaving what you call well or badly, spiritually or mortally. In fact, they need more Love and Guidance when they have strayed off the path of peace. Help Me to help them by becoming a Channel for my Light to reach them.

Blessings to you all, my straying children.

SHINING YOUR LIGHT

My Children, rise above your feelings of fear and despondency. Know that I am with you and all people all over your world.

You keep being shown the horror and devastation of war on your TV screens and it is right that you remember constantly all those who are suffering, but do not let it 'get you down'. At least you who are praying and using the Light and Love which surrounds you are helping. And helping so much more than you realise.

Rise above your fears and anxieties. Keep holding all peoples in My Love and Care.

Push out the pictures that come to your minds of things that have not happened. Terror does not have power. Make Peace and Love so strong in your minds and in your sending out of them that evil sinks to its nothingness. Evil has no power.

All Leaders in ALL countries need your help and guidance. When you pray you are sending them MY help and guidance. No one person on their own wishes to experience terror and death.

Deep inside everyone of you is a longing for a peaceful, happy life, a life with comfort and food, friends. Those you think of as enemies have the same basic needs and feelings as you. You are all one, but you forget this.

Great waves of power are being circulated all around my children, wherever they are.

Those of you who so want Peace, know that it is with you now, everywhere. It is already there. Know it, then send forth that knowing of peace and love to your so-called enemies. Also hold the leaders of all countries in the Light of Peace. They can feel it.

Because you all have free will you know that great, unthinkable catastrophes can happen, but they do not have to. Do not make realities of them by picturing, imagining them.

See peace and love filtering through to ALL people everywhere. You are all ONE. Do not try to give power to fear and terrorism.

A tiny shaft of light beamed into a dark cave can penetrate the seeming darkness; make that slit, or crack bigger and bigger and the light grows more and more until finally every dark corner of that cave is lit. The light shows that the darkness was nothing, no thing. That hole was only seeming space, but the light turns it into something you can see. You could not 'see' the darkness, but you can see the light. Use it.

Use it with love many times a day. You know now how to do that and the more of you that do it, the more the darkness disappears, for it was a lack of something, which was Light.

You have been given free will, but you have also been given great power. Use it for Good.

I never leave you – any of you.

136

Here I will insert a beautiful message given to someone who was about to start a great work for humanity:

> "I have given everyone a cross to bear, some heavy, some not so heavy.
>
> I will give you the spiritual strength to carry theirs – and whilst you do this for me, I will carry yours."

NEGATIVE NEWS

18.12.01

Dear God, I am tired of all the bad news, the negative news, the pictures of war and destruction. In my heart I believe there is an improvement in world conditions – a move towards a better life. Please give us an uplifting message to raise our spirit and strengthen our endeavours for world peace.

There is a weariness amongst many of my people. They wonder and doubt how much good they do by their prayers and positive thinking. There is a heaviness in many of your hearts because, even though you may not have a relative in the armed forces, you think of the feelings of those who have. In a way you carry their load.

Now the best way you can help all people, in all countries, is by visualising true Peace. You are learning that when you choose for something, it happens. Choose now for Peace, for understanding, for leadership-guidance. Choose for peace and love to be manifested amongst all my children. Deep in their hearts, in your hearts, all long for true Peace.

You must remember that in the hearts of those that you think of as enemies, as destructionists, there is the same longing for peace, a feeling of safety.

Those of you who pray regularly really do build up a great wall of Light, a layer of Light. See this spreading in all directions in all places. Hold the forces of war in this Light, hold the starving and homeless in this Light. See the women and children being fed and clothed, indeed all people being led into the new age of glory. It is nearer than you think.

Do not allow yourselves to become despondent – there is no need. Be pleased that you can help. If you helped just one soul would you not think your effort worthwhile? Well, I tell you, you are helping thousands upon thousands to experience a new life. A life of peace and plenty beyond their dreams.

Never give up. Keep on 'knowing the Truth' which is that I am with each one of you, my children, at all times. It is my wish and my desire that you all be happy, healthy, wealthy and wise. You are already, but you do not accept this knowledge which is deep within you.

To all those of you who hear my voice, hear me now – I wish you a wonderful Christ Mass.

— 2002 —

WORLD TURMOIL

I seem to be in that mood again of doubting I shall 'hear' the right message. I need a message of encouragement for all of us who are making a big effort to help our planet while it is in such a state of turmoil.

Peace, my children. Quiet that fretful, busy daily mind which is constantly being fed, through the media, with world turmoil and unrest.

Look for improvements instead of trouble. Many situations are not as bad as you feared.

Fear is still so strong amongst my people, but those of you who know the power of prayer and love can do so much, indeed are doing so much, to allay fear. Tremendous power is being generated by the strength of your prayers for peace. World leaders are feeling this power of peace; the wanting of revenge is diminishing and the thoughts of peace and love are taking the place of the thoughts of revenge.

Keep shining that Great Light of Peace and Love over the countries fearing war and destruction. You can do so much with your right thoughts. I keep telling you this, but you keep doubting. Why?

You do not believe that you are so powerful, that you can alter situations with your thoughts. YOU CAN. Deep within, all my children want peace and love; the women and children long for it, the men have forgotten how satisfying it is. Many of the men still consider fighting to be Manly; well it is – women do not desire that feeling and they wish the men would feel as they do. As I have said before, the women and children need your gentle, positive thoughts, the men need your strong, powerful thoughts that can annihilate their feelings of revenge.

Notice the improvements, the shifts towards peace, the 'giving in' of some of the rebels. The Good is multiplying fast – look for it. Never lose hope, never stop knowing how powerful you are for Good to overcome your self-inflicted evil.

Now is the time to pray for all people to be satisfied, not always wanting more – more land, more wealth, more, more, more. Those of you who are happiest are those who are content with their lot, their place on the planet, their blessings. Count your blessings, even though they may seem very few, count them and you will find that miraculously they increase. See Good, feel Love around you, give out kindness and consideration. Be forgiving at all times, try to understand why some people are like they are and give out extra love to them, even though that seems difficult.

Expect more positive output from your media; expect to hear more from those who know in their hearts that conditions can be improved by better use of your land, by caring about the results of its treatment. Do not give power to those who are greedy for profits and careless of the effect on their brothers. Wars are not being fought only with guns and weapons, they are being fought with pesticides, animal cruelty, greed for more and more output from less land. There is enough for all. When will you realise that?

You do not know the satisfaction of a 'job well done' – well a few of you do, but there is need for a big swing towards selflessness.

Do not be despondent. From our higher viewpoint we can see the Good that is being achieved by your prayers, your faith, your love. These weapons are much stronger than guns, bombs and threats. Put that cloak of Love over all your world, knowing that it is so strong it can withstand all negative matter.

Be strong in your hearts. Know that I know all the good that is in your hearts and I will gather it up and multiply it for the good of all. Do not doubt my dear ones. You are my beautiful children and I love you.

PROOF OF LIFE AFTER DEATH

Will you please give me a message for those who say to me, "I'd like to believe there is something after death, but there is no proof."

Why do you think it is too frivolous to write down what you have just 'seen'?

[To tune-in I pictured the dove grey velvet and the pink rose bud and I thought I was 'out of my mind' when the rose bud lifted its head and winked at me with a smile on its face. It seemed to be saying 'We know, don't we, that there is no death'.] Now some readers will think I am a nut case.

Do you think people are more impressed with continual seriousness? Do you still believe that death is so dramatic, so sad, that it cannot be smiled about?

No, I don't think that, but most people are a bit shocked when I talk about it confidently, with no sign of fear or doubt. And sometimes I am somewhat flippant about it.

Have you ever stood at X-roads and wondered which way to go? You have no idea; you are in a foreign land; you cannot understand the sign posts.

Yes, I did exactly that in Europe and can visualise the place now.

Well you must have found your way around because you returned safely to your ship. You gave thought to the situation and worked things out for yourself and you made mental notes so that, when returning, you remembered the way back more easily.

You had several choices for that experience. You could have studied a map first, you could have waited around for someone to ask who could speak your language, you could have panicked.

These people who ask you about death and its outcome – they have choices. If they really wish to receive an answer to their question they can listen to those of you who have no doubts, who have read and studied and experienced their own answers; they can have a real desire to find out more and the right books and articles will find them; they can choose to go on doubting or not think about it at all, or they can say, "I don't think we are supposed to know, it is a mystery. I have tried to live a good life; I have helped others where I could and I just leave it at that."

Now that attitude is fine. So long as they have no fear, they are living in the NOW. But if there is a little niggling fear that is pushed out of the way, but has a habit of cropping up at times, then it is a pity if they do not dare to open their hearts to someone else, or open the pages of books that come their way, or go deep within and start to give some thought to their wonderings.

In the stillness of their deepest feelings they will find comfort. They will remember their real Being, they will feel its indestructableness.

There is only one thing that all of you know without a doubt and that is, at some time, you will die. You take trouble finding out about different illnesses and their effects on your bodies; you study stars, you learn about past civilisations, but so many of you do not want to study death. It is

141

something you do not want to think about or prepare for. You know why? Because you are afraid of it. You have been given the wrong 'pictures'. You think of the dead, useless overcoat, you see the hearse, the coffin, the grave. You torment yourselves with gloom and grief.

Now I am speaking to those of you that do this. And most of you that do this would not admit it to your closest and dearest, nor to anyone if you could avoid it.

What a pity, I am not suggesting that you spend your lives looking forward to dying. Oh, no. But you can give it as much thought as is healthy. It is not a closed book, not to be looked at occasionally, and planned for with intelligence. Why leave it to others to wonder, after you have departed, what you would really like to happen to your remains and your affairs?

You have such a glorious future in front of you. You will experience such joy. Imagine what you will like to experience, who you will like to meet, what you will like to learn. Then put that picture to one-side. Just look at it occasionally to refresh your memory for when the time comes.

Have no fear, just know the truth – that there is no death. You are never NOT!

RELIGIOUS BIGOTRY

Why do the Protestants and Catholics hate each other so much in Northern Ireland?

Your religions all think they are 'right'. Have I not told you this many times before? There is Truth in all of them and error in all of them.

I repeat, it does not matter how you pray or dress or chant. If it helps, do it, but do not expect everyone else to do likewise.

If what you practise makes you feel nearer to Me, Truth, then do it. But I tell you this, it makes no difference to your connection with me. You are never apart from me.

You saw on your television screens recently the children from a Protestant school and from a Catholic school meeting on a pathway and then proceeding in twos to walk along another path. Take that as a wonderful example of how they should be encouraged to bridge that gap.

Keep cats and dogs separated in large groups, then when they meet they fight. Keep them under the same roof and they live happily together.

Put black and white children together at a young age and they do not notice the difference between them, for in truth there is no difference.

Love needs to be nurtured at an early age in all my children. Love, compassion, loyalty, peace.

These natural attributes are instinctive to the very young. Their outlook can be warped by example. Do you not see how important it is to start teaching your children new values? You cannot call yourselves adult while you set such bad examples. All conflict is caused because you do not understand that you are all One. What you do to others, you do to yourselves.

It is by your example you teach most and this applies not just to teachers, but very much to parents.

How many people do you see reading to learn? Much of what they read is similar to what they watch – it is OK for entertainment, but not for hours and hours, filling your minds with clutter.

Add these thoughts to your prayers – that little children will be brought up to better understand how they should behave to be happy and to make others happy.

Thoughtfulness is not very high up on your curricula at any stage of your lives, from babyhood, through school, to college. Prune your bushes to allow for new growth, cut out the old, damaged, dead wood that has served its purpose. Make room for the new.

Why did I not 'hear' anything yesterday?

By not hearing did it not make you do quite a lot of thinking?

Yes. I thought quite a lot about being sure I became a clear channel. I thought about the necessity of 'clearing my atmosphere'!

You have your answer.

LOSS OF A CHILD

21.1.02

I have just been watching a TV programme showing the terrible grief that is felt by parents when they lose a child, whether it be a baby of a few days old or an older child. There seems no real comfort to offer them. How do YOU comfort them dear God?

They are never alone, nor is the little one that has gone from their sight, temporarily.

We talked about grief recently; this is a very deep grief, only given to those who are strong enough to bear it.

This is an experience for both the parents and the child or children. They have to be very strong to be given this seeming burden. I am with them at all times and I know all that is taking place. Can you understand that those parents will never be the same earthly people again? They have experienced a supreme pain.

The physical pain, the tears, the feeling of devastation is important to experience, but even more important is the sacrifice they have made for their earthly brethren. By their grief and their example, their fortitude, their faith, they are being a tower of strength to others – others who do not even begin to know how to comfort them.

There are times when this devastation brings my children back to me, both the parents and the onlookers. I know it is hard for you to understand that nothing happens by chance, but there is a great lesson here and only those who have reached a high level of spirituality can benefit and remember from this.

You are never given more pain then you can bear, you are never given more sorrow than you can bear. It may seem like it at the time, but you become 'better' people by your suffering.

Have we not talked about not being able to help others if you have not experienced what they experience, be it pain, loss, extreme poverty, extreme fear?

For those of you who do not know what to say to the bereaved, may I remind you of a previous talk. It is sufficient to say, "What can I do to help you?" or "Do you want to talk about it?" or "I have some lovely books that you might find helpful."

If you will turn to Me at all times you will find Me there to comfort you and guide you. I never leave you alone.

STATE OF THE WORLD

I feel bleak. The weather is cold and grey; publishers keep returning the extracts I send in of YOUR work. How am I going to get this lovely teaching to others? Nobody seems to want to do anything about the state of the world.

Aren't they concerned? We are heading for disaster unless we get together and make almighty efforts to pray for Peace.

Where am I going wrong, dear God?

Are you forgetting to be positive? Are you Choosing for more to be done for your planet? You are shown so much negativity through your media.

There is so much greed and discontent being displayed. Our education, health and transport systems are in a mess. Crime and violence are all around. Is it natural for some of us to be discontented and despondent?

It does not help any situation when you give way to despondency. Are you remembering to hold your media in the Light?

No, I forgot you had mentioned that earlier on. There is so much we forget, which brings me to asking – why is it that we listen to or read your wonderful words, yet we cannot remember them, even shortly afterwards? We want to go on feeling their hope and wisdom, we want to relax in their comfort. But we all say 'I can't remember that later'. On re-reading the CWG books, even after many times, most of it comes anew as we re-read your lovely words.

You take in more than you realise. You fill your freezers with food – it is all there for when you need it, but you soon forget what you put there to freeze. But nothing stops you from opening the door and looking in. 'Oh yes,' you think, 'all this food is there for my use as I need it.' Some days you require one item, another day you require quite a different item. Is that not so?

145

Yes, I love it when you give these analogies. It makes sense and is simplicity. And is it right that we don't need this 'food' all the time? We get it out to help ourselves and others to be nourished?

Your household freezer is confined to a small space and requires de-frosting from time to time. Your etheric freezer is limitless in size and needs no de-frosting. You can never overload it, but there is only so much you can place in it at a time or it would become all jumbled up. There are compartments and there is order in these freezers both kinds. You do not take out vegetables for a sweet course, nor ice cream to make a savoury. So with your soul mind, you take out what is required at the time, but unlike your material freezer, your soul freezer can have anything you take out returned to it. There are no sell-by dates!

What would I take out to help the victims of earthquakes; those who are made homeless, without anything in the way of possessions?

You are thinking in terms of right words, are you not? You, yourself, cannot physically go to their aid, but use your greatest power – prayer. Pray for them to be rescued and helped, see aid going to them, make a reality of it. Then there are those who are able who will give of themselves physically to deliver help and those who will give of their worldly goods, be it money, food, clothes. Pray that all human kind will feel that wonderful gift known as compassion and expressed as giving. It will happen. Make it happen with your thoughts and prayers.

When you have a box of fireworks you do not let off all the large ones at once. A lot of small ones are handed out to the children. Now compare this with what is going on in your world. There are the great eruptions, the major wars, the devastating weapons, then there are the petty crimes, the street squabbles, the lesser crimes.

We can see the improvements that you are not shown. Look for the improvements, look for the wisdom now being expressed by some leaders. Do not feel 'bleak', never give up hope and optimism.

See the great rose tree from which that beautiful bud has come – know there are millions of buds waiting to open the hearts of all humankind, especially my little children that are being born again on to the earth plane. Prepare the soil so that they may flourish as they grow, without all the trauma that you have been making for yourselves for so many centuries. You were created for peace and love, not for war and famine.

Bless you all. Think deeply.

MOTIVATION

28.1.02

I feel I need a good shove to get me going again with this work. I anticipated using the winter months to type out pages of Your knowledge, but I seem to have run out of questions because most of the answers are already in Neale's and others' books. Where am I going adrift?

You know that I know your every thought. You know that I know your every hope. You know that I know you, the real you, better than anyone else knows you.

You know that I have told you we do not waste our resources. You know that I have told you this work is not just for you and that you are to get it published.

In your heart you know that you are being tested. Always remember what your very good friend told you – your determination and enthusiasm have got you through all your seeming difficulties all your life. Now go and think about all this. Fill yourself with positive, happy thoughts and re-experience your determination and enthusiasm. Let it shine forth. I am watching you and listening to you at all times. You know that and you do not mind, except I could say you should mind more!

29.1.02

It has taken me half an hour to 'tune-in' this morning – I wonder why? There is scarcely a sound after yesterday's terrific gale and the sun is shining.

My mortal mind kept flitting around. Now I am inside the pink rose bud. I can feel the softness of its petals against my face and I can see the flow from its gold stamens. Right in the centre is a many-faceted small diamond. What is this telling me, dear God?

You are now experiencing perfect Peace, all quiet, Oneness with your real self. This is the part of you that is completeness. You wish for nothing more while you are in this state. You can hold this State of Being for as long as you wish, but do you wish to remain like this?

What purpose am I serving in this State?

You are resting, you are charging your atoms, although you cannot feel anything. You are absorbing the Light. Now you can fly away, taking the Light, as a butterfly leaves a rose and flies off to another part of the garden.

You are free as the air, as light as a feather, as carefree as a moment in time.

But you cannot, nor do you wish to remain in this State. It is not in your present nature to remain so. You wish to turn the page, to see what is round the corner, to meet up with other moments. This is natural for the stage at which you are.

My children are all moving, never static. Some are remembering, some are learning, some are teaching.

Close your rose bud, knowing that you have absorbed its essence into your Being. Return to earth. I will find work for you to do.

Seal yourself back into your earthly body. You know how to do that. Remember when you do your Noon work that you are just one of thousands doing the same thing. One grain of salt may seem minute, but pick up a spoonful and think of the difference.

There are many souls around you on a higher plane, not only helping and guiding you, but there are those that are learning from you and picking up your thoughts because it is easier for them to do this at the stage at which they find themselves. Some of them knew you on earth and can 'hear' your teaching and now understand it better than they could while they wore their earthly garments. There is great love around you my child.

Do not cry – just be elated. Bless you.

THOUGHT IN ACTION

I have put a small brush into each of your hands, filled with gold paint. What picture will you paint?

Onto a midnight blue sky as a background, I paint buildings of all descriptions. There are beautiful domes, minarets, churches, tower blocks, small houses. I know that all these buildings are filled with people.

There is a wonderful glow from all these buildings. I wonder why I have painted all these religious buildings? I know that it is not necessary to have these places to reach you, God. I know that you are right where I am and where everyone is. If the paint had not been gold I am sure I would have painted a country scene of trees and fields. Why is this so?

You have been 'conditioned' all your life to connect holy things, prayer, opulence, plenty, wealth, with gold.

Had I put silver paint in the brushes you would probably have painted Love, in the way of Cupid, musical notes, again churches.

Different colours would have brought forth different scenes. You could have quite a game in this way, working with red or grey or yellow.

You become 'conditioned' by what you are told and what you read as you grow up and this 'colours' your whole life.

Whatever is the lesson here? I cannot see where we are going!

I am making you show yourself what your imagination can do. You could play this 'game' by mentally touching satin, velvet, sacking, fur, concrete. Then you could use scents, from fried onions to orange peel or lilies or sweet peas. Now try sounds. Thunder, guns, bells, violins, a choir boy's voice, a skylark.

Yes, I see and hear all that as you speak, but where are we going?

You are experiencing the power of Thought. You are seeing thought in action.

Now put this in a different context. You use all these senses as you do your prayer-work. You form pictures in your minds at all times. Your words form the pictures and the pictures form your words.

Let your Mind make your prayers real; run into your mind instead of away from it. Make realities. You do this, but you do not realise how powerful you are Being. Think about this lesson, this talk. It is deep, not nonsensical. Now do your Noon work child.

Bless you and all my children who are working so faithfully to help your planet.

When I went to do my work, I picked up my little White Eagle booklet called "The Source of All Our Strength" and, as usual, it opened at a right place to verify and help me with the lesson I had just received!

WHAT'S IN A NAME?

2.2.02

The picture of the pink rose bud against the grey velvet appears to have an indistinct signature in gold at the bottom of the right-hand corner.

What does it read?

It is difficult to see. I think it says 'Guiding Star' with a line under it, like the line I draw under my signature today.

And does this bring back memories?

Yes, many years ago I was told that was my name in a North American incarnation and I thought it a lovely name. Another time I was known, in that country, as Moon Flower, my husband was Moon Cloud and his father was Moon Rake.

You recall rightly. Which name do you prefer now?

I like the implication of Guiding Star, but it seems rather presumptuous.

Are you back to belittling yourself?

Perhaps.

Do you think that name suits you now?

Not until I get this work published and of use to others. Then I like to think it may guide some souls to a better way of thinking about life. And I wonder why I was called that so long ago? What did I do then to warrant that name?

Let us just say you helped others along their path. You will understand more when you remember more at a later, higher level of your existence.

I don't think I shall wish this to be published.

Putting yourself down again?

Well, I don't feel all that useful at the moment. I feel inadequate. We are so puny compared with the forces of nature. Does it do us any good to watch all these programmes about storms, hurricanes, volcanic eruptions?

You saw something interesting recently, didn't you? Scientists were amazed to have discovered a civilisation that appeared to have lived without boundaries and without using weapons. Does that not teach you all something important?

It should do. We know we should not and need not fight each other if only we will be satisfied with our space and practise loving each other.

There is a beginning, or rather a reversion, to a golden age of peace. You are feeling the birth pangs at the moment, but it is as a moment in Time, then all will be Peace once more. Look forward, never backward, and know that My Will will be Done and you will know how it is in Heaven.

TECHNOPHOBIA

27.2.02

You know, dear God, how I have been putting off this first tune-in with you on my new computer. Why? I drove my new car for the first time with hardly a qualm, but this seems so much more difficult. The booklet I have just looked at might as well be in Latin.

Do not feel so helpless and hopeless. You have been longing for a way to get this work to people everywhere. Do you not think your dear sons were guided to procure this new instrument for you? Heed some of the thoughts that are now coming to you; new ideas for 'broadcasting' my words. Do I need to tell you again, we do not waste our resources? Remove your worry beads – they are inappropriate.

You all need to see the good in yourselves and love yourselves before you can see the good in each other and love each other, without criticism or judgment. Put your own house in order before you try to tell others how to put theirs in order.

I am finding it hard to keep the contact. Shall I stop for now?

You can see your rose has opened – that should give you joy. I know it is still lying down, but the day is nearer when you will see it standing upright. Now have a good old practice with your new machine.

151

It is depressing to see more and more fighting between men; not only between countries, but between those in their own countries and always in the name of religion. It makes religion lose all meaning. Please explain, dear God.

You see a mental picture of legs and feet trying to walk through rough undergrowth. It is hard-going because there are brambles, thorns, sharp pieces of wood, thickets.

This is what man has done with his religion. Instead of the smooth, soft path that is there for all to tread, so many obstacles have been put in the way. So much has grown there for such a long time that the roots are deep. Gone are the simple little flowers.

It will take centuries of your time to clear this strong growth, but as you move forward you come to open spaces where the sunlight is able to shine through. Groups are sitting around, contented and knowing they have made progress; knowing they have come through the rough, painful trail and can now look forward.

Mainly comparatively few can see the distance, they are resting from their trials. Some are moving forward, knowing there is a beautiful goal to reach. No money is required, no buildings need to be erected, no rules have to be left en route for those who will follow. Those going ahead have dropped off all the weight they were carrying. They do not really wish to look back at the old path. The new one is so much easier and the little children are so happy to follow where they are being led.

All discord has gone, all noise, and the air is so pure. Negativity has been dropped off. Here is great love abounding, with everyone in harmony, knowing the path they have found is so easy and they feel great Peace. As night comes they sit in large circles and listen to those who wish to pass on their thoughts; thoughts of the Allness.

Thought is manifesting and all their simple needs are met. This state is heaven on earth my children. All are One and there are no boundaries, only a way ahead.

This has been a wonderful 'walk' and I want to be on it, but it does not appeal to those who are remaining in their own quagmire. They still feel so right in what they do and who they slay. Oh , I can see how important it is to stop making weapons, to be satisfied with what we have. To put into practice all you are telling us. I know you can send us more Teachers; why do you give us so few?

There are those of you who want to go forward and those of you who do not want to believe. There are so many who wish to hang on to what they have been taught. Liken it to you, yourself, being reluctant to let go of your old computer because you thought you knew that way better. Now you are coming into more light; you are finding more short cuts; the new way is becoming clear. Believe me, there are enough teachers for those who wish to listen and remember and learn. There are enough books, enough examples. They come to you when you are ready.

I can only implore you to pray and to talk to those who will listen. Re-read what you have already found. There are millions of you on this bright path. Meet up with them. See Truth rising into the sky like a great fountain and falling all over your earth. It will not go completely ignored.

DEALING WITH CRIMINALS

6.3.02

They were such beautiful pages I read yesterday from Neale Donald Walsch's "Friendship with God" – all about loving and letting each one go their own way. It made sense until I tried to apply it in my mind to the young thug who has been on remand forty times. He shows no remorse and wears a cynical smile. People who live around him fear to go out at night. I wondered, when watching that documentary, what Jesus would have said to him.

When Jesus is said to have cast out sin, he was really letting in Light. When only a curtain keeps out the Light it is easy to pull it aside; when it is a brick wall it takes longer to drill through. When it is a great thick flint or stone wall it takes longest of all to make even a tiny hole.

The wall is full of resistance. Flogging it would have no effect at all. You thought of a good flogging, didn't you?

Yes, yet I knew that wouldn't be a permanent cure.

And it would bring out the worst in the one who was doing the flogging. They would experience a feeling of revenge.

These souls feel the world owes them something. They have not been shown love nor any joy in giving and receiving.

153

Am I right in feeling that they need endless patience and non-judgmental love on a one-to-one basis, explaining to them how to enjoy life, how to choose for what they are looking. Though none of that would help if they are on drugs.

Many of you are on drugs in varying degrees. You smoke, you take tablets, you believe that they are somehow doing you good. Well, in a way tablets do help you because you believe they can take away your pain. Your pain is not real, but it appears to be because you believe. There is no brain in a bone or a muscle or a cut that is able to tell your Intelligence that it hurts. Most of you experience aches and pains, some very severe, that you do not know how else to deal with, other than by taking something that enables you to ignore them.

But how did those hurts get there in the first place? You think you are at the mercy of something or someone that causes you pain, either bodily or mentally or psychologically. The real cure comes to you when you start to understand the cause. This can be as simple as the fact of stealing because you want something, to the much more complicated experience of hurting because you have let someone else invade your territory, either materially or mentally. The deeper the seeming hurt, the longer it takes to eradicate it.

This is where true Healers can help. They require endless patience, great love and a deep understanding of their fellow men. They are about, as are the Teachers we talked about recently. Who is going to start the ball rolling in the right direction? Who is going to be brave enough to tackle these difficult problems – incidentally all brought on by yourselves through lack of Love.

It sounds such a gigantic task.

Do you think it will take as long as trying to find Peace by fighting and bombing and quarrelling? Thirty years and more some of these 'cures' have been going on, causing death, destruction, maimed people, devastated women and children. All hope and comfort being taken away from innocent onlookers.

Sometimes you spend a long time mixing a cake, then you put it in the oven and forget. What use is the result of your labours? And all because you forgot to think, to remember.

All that makes sense, but it has not been uplifting. It gives me that bleak feeling about humankind. It makes me feel guilty that I can be 'happy, healthy, wealthy and wise', amidst this chaos. Now I will go and do 'my twelve o'clock' and pray for all these poor souls.

FEAR

There is so much Fear around at this time. My children are afraid of the storms, the floods, the airways, inflation, low interest rates, unemployment; then on a wider scale, wars, violence, terrorism, destruction and death.

You give away your freedom through greed, speed, 'weed' and alcoholism. Who are those you know that are happy? Are they not those who are satisfied, not always wanting, wanting for more? You have free will and free choice. When will you remember to use those precious gifts wisely?

Do you know, the children that are being born now are wonderful messengers of Truth. They require careful nurturing, encouragement to speak their minds. But firstly, they need a good example from you at the start of their return lives. They do not all need to all learn all things. In other words, they know what subjects appeal to them for the work they will do in their futures. Other than the three Rs as you call them, they will gravitate to the knowledge they will require and which will rekindle in them what it is they have come to teach You.

And your joy can be in telling them there is no need for war, fighting, grabbing for other people's belongings. Some of you have never experienced the joy of giving and sharing. There really is so much joy in giving. Then when you do receive, you experience what is in the heart of the giver.

Haven't those of you who are parents told of the joy your child has found in it's most basic, cheapest toy compared with the costly ones? The most priceless gift you can give your children is Love.

Clean up your television programmes, your advertisements, your language and your Minds.

You like the fairy stories all your life; the good winning, the happy-ever-after ending. And your lives can be as fairy stories, and not just with a happy ending, but with a happy living.

155

I am deeply interested in home education since watching a programme about it. Will it become a thing of the future?

I indicated to you recently that a different type of being is re-incarnating now. There will be the same free choice for them, but they will be choosing to be more thinking souls with a strong parental instinct –they will be more interested in their children's welfare, thus wanting more say in their upbringing and education. You will see more examples of the joy this brings.

How will they be able to afford to stay home, where will their income come from?

Do you recall our talk about the saving in money if military power was scrapped? How there would be enough wealth to feed and house all the starving of the world. Well, there would be a similar saving if many schools and colleges were scrapped, enough to make good payments to parents, with some left over to employ specialist teachers to spend a few hours weekly with certain subjects. There would still be facilities for those who wanted mass education, but most children, if given their choice, would choose to be at home, learning from those they love and specialising in their favourite subjects.

All this cannot happen quickly. As you say, Rome was not built in a day – although looking on it seems like that to us! No, my children, there is just a beginning. Remember how you enjoyed teaching your small son when you were in Africa and how you were told he was two years ahead when you returned to England.? Then remember what both sons learned from their father – to such an extent that a special subject was added to their curriculum.

How many people are really happy in their work? Pressure is put upon them, stress is experienced, all because of Greed – more and more is wanted so as to gain more and more profit. And who is really happy? Why, those of you who are satisfied with your lot.

You have much food for thought – and sufficient food for your bodies without spending more than you earn to buy yourselves your needs. And you will not feel deprived; nay, you will feel complete and nourished and healthy in mind and body.

Go away and think! Bless you all.

LIVING IN PEACE & HARMONY

You have explained to us how to live in peace and harmony; that what we experience is up to us; we have free will and free choice, but, oh, it is depressing how far away we are from that state. There is conflict all over the world and now so much in our little country, which was once a safe and peaceful place. Even our children are unruly and uncontrollable, defying the police, threatening, violent, full of hate.

Tie up a dog, starve it of food, show it no affection, kick out at it and what happens? It snaps and snarls at all who go near it, biting, growling because it has never been shown love or been cared for. It is afraid of all around it including everybody.

These children you see, do you think they have been brought up in a loving home, cared for and talked to? Do you think they have been watched and guided in all their ways? And when they go to school, are they guided and taught to love one another? Their teachers are afraid of them and they pick up this fear and add it to what they already felt.

Not only the deprived and disadvantaged behave badly and feel unloved, the rich employ others to teach and control their children while they follow their own selfish pursuits. Then those children become dissatisfied and want more, more. What kind of example are parents, and all adults, being to children?

You all need Love, my children. You feel so different when you are loved, when you are encouraged, when you are able to speak what is on your minds, or about what is worrying you. Think of the joy of being with some friends, teachers, neighbours, who show kindness, freely and lovingly. You become lifted up.

Many of you are learning the hard way because of your thoughtlessness. You rarely witness birds or mammals quarrelling – and when they do they are defending their territory or their mate or their young. You can see their love for their young, their selflessness in feeding them, often going hungry themselves. This is true of many of my children, but unfortunately they do not make the headlines, until there are thousands of them.

You would do well to understand the meaning of words like equality, thoughtfulness, example, gentleness, fairness. Then to realise the power of Love, Prayer, Giving. Then there is the contagion of laughter, happiness, truthfulness, honesty, trust. Mainly your priorities are not only poor, but missing on your list for living a happy existence. You are your own worst enemies. Take heed of those who are happy and contented. Would you not like to be like them?

A long time ago, we talked about competition. About it not being so important who won a race, but that all enjoyed the experience. It really does not matter one iota if your friend has more pencils than you do, more expensive gear, a bigger house. You might happen to notice that he has less friends or less good health or more loneliness. You could add to the list of words to study 'compassion, awareness, true understanding, unselfishness',

Put down your mechanical arms and stretch out your bodily arms – open them wide. You never know what wonderful item you will catch or save and your inner feeling would be indescribable.

Think more, pray more. Pray for understanding amongst all people. By your thinking you can slow down or speed up your experience of Utopia.

LIFE AFTER DEATH (III)

Sometimes I long for important questions to ask; other times I think of comparatively unimportant questions just out of curiosity. For instance, do we get tired on our next plane of existence?

You will not feel physically tired as you do on your present planet, nor experience aches and pains, but you will reach what you describe as absorption point, when you have taken in as much as you can digest at a given point.

I believe we shall truly tax our understanding, but how will we exercise our bodies with work? If everything happens through thought, why would we need to do gardening? Do flowers die and are there weeds?

You will desire to alter your gardens, to change your flowers, to experiment with grafting and cuttings. You will re-design, re-create. All this you will do with thought, with your minds. Your much lighter bodies will not need strenuous exercise.

A carpenter, a painter, a musician, will use that wonderful tool you call imagination. You will build a house without bricks, make a chair without wood, sow a lawn without seed. All is MIND. You cannot now build a house without a design nor make a chair without a preconceived idea. We have talked about instantaneous thought. In your present state you cannot think of anything without 'seeing' it, be it a postage stamp or a daisy. Try it!

Will we sleep?

Not in the way you now think of sleep, as being an unconsciousness. You are not unconscious now when you sleep – you are elsewhere.

I am aware of this now. I have caught myself 'coming back into my body', as if I didn't quite make it in time.

That is exactly what death is. It is no more than leaving your body and instead of coming back into it, you stay where you are, usually in a much more acceptable place!

That is exactly what I know deep within me and it is a comforting thought. Oh, how I wish I could make the unbelievers believe this.

Remember about free choice? You would be imposing your will on another.

I just don't like people being afraid of death.

They do not need to choose to be afraid. Deep inside all my children is Truth.

Do animals fear death?

Animals fear being caught. Animals do not fear their natural death. They use instinct and heed it.

Is it true that meat-eaters take into their own bodies the fear of the animals that have lined up to be slaughtered? If so, are vegetarians more compassionate and less belligerent?

Do you think it is kind to eat your brother animals? Do you think your brother animals deserve to be slaughtered, made to suffer fear? Yes, you do absorb their fear into your own bodies. My children are inconsistent. They mend a bird's wing, then shoot it down when it is flying. They help a hedgehog across a road, yet kill a cow.

All my children can become more compassionate and less belligerent if they will think more deeply.

That answers the question, continually on my mind, as to why there is so much dreadful fighting amongst human beings all over the world. Life seems to have no meaning and the deaths men are causing bring such misery to others, especially women and children. Surely we are all becoming fearful for the future?

Fear, Greed, Selfishness. The panacea is Love, Giving, Selflessness. The choice is yours.

That seems almost as if you do not care, you do not choose to help us!

My Guidance and my Love are always with you. You do not have to pay lawyers' fees to receive help. I give you freely all that you need and much more than you need. How can I help you if you do not ask and listen? How can I speak to you and show you the way when you shut your eyes and your ears? How can you help yourselves when you do not go deep within to find the Truth. Your Survival Instinct does not require you to kill another! That answers several of your queries, does it not?

HEAVENLY STATUS
9.4.02

I have been watching the funeral service of our Queen Mother, Elizabeth. I wondered what it must be like for her when she arrives back on the other side. She has been used to being someone so revered, so elevated, yet I know we are all equal. Does that tremendous love that has been given out to her help to 'put her somewhat apart' when she returns 'home'?

Those who have led unselfish, exemplary lives while on the earth plane, be they monks or monarchs, find themselves in 'suitable' surroundings.

You would not place a sixth-former in a kindergarten nor a nun with a pop group, not initially. You would surround them with others with whom they would feel comfortable and at ease. However, you all have lessons to learn or remember and if it benefits you to be with complete opposites, then you will , in time, choose to be with those of Unlike kind.

We have talked about not being able to help those who have experienced great sorrow or pain if you have not suffered likewise. You are ever evolving, experiencing, living your life, not only for your benefit, but for the benefit of others.

I have told you, you have no need to bow or kneel to Me, so you will not feel the need to do this to others. You are all equal and your aim is to become 'more equal'.

There are no boundaries to Love, no boundaries to Fear nor to elation and joy.

You may need to learn to appreciate music or beauty, but there is no limit or exception that keeps some souls on the outside looking in.

Some may prefer to wear sackcloth and grow daisies rather than wear silk and grow orchids. Many of your earthly values are irrelevant when you rise to higher thinking and evolving.

A dog would rather have a bone than a bow; a tiger would rather experience freedom than live in a cage, even though thousands of people were looking on and admiring him. You, yourself, would rather live in a cottage than a palace. Then there is the choice of preferring plain bread and butter to adding jam and cream.

Some of my children feel near me in a great cathedral, others in a garden. You do not require material things to make you contented and happy.

The Love that has been shown this day strengthens and raises the spirit of those who would mourn. Love is prayer and prayer is love.

GROWING OLD

I am amazed to learn that not only do people fear death and dying, but growing old, even when they are only young. Is it conceit? Do they see old people as ugly? I know I have wrinkles, but I have not noticed if I have frown lines. You will not judge I know, but I would like to hear what you say.

You can see your rosebud settling down to sleep because it knows it is perfect and does not wish to enter into this dialogue! You know your rosebud tells you a lot, doesn't it?

This is another example of my children not being satisfied with what they have. Would they choose to all look alike? Do they wish to look 'bland'? They cannot see themselves as others see them and certainly not as I see them.

The face of your baby or your pet is beautiful to you. As they think, as they love, as they grow they alter because circumstances are forming their earth lives. Hardship, cruelty, sadness leave their mark, but so do joy, love and selflessness. You look what you are and though you try to remove the lines, you cannot alter the expression in the eyes.

161

A great old tree is more appealing than a sapling, yet a rose bud can seem more beautiful than a full blown bloom. All is movement. There is beauty in a still, calm being, whether it be a flower or a face, but there is much beauty in animation.

It is interesting to see how you use your free choice. You cannot give advice to others who are set in their ways. It means nothing to say "if I were you", but it means much to say "if you were me". Judge not. You can look on and marvel at another's choice, but do not try to take it away.

You have a saying, "There is nothing right or wrong, but thinking makes it so". Think about that.

TRUST

Why is it taking me so long to learn how to use this new computer? Is it to do with age, which doesn't really exist, or do I not concentrate enough?

You have just seen your rose stand up, then lie down in the opposite direction. What is that telling you?

That I am looking at a new and different picture; the rose and the velvet are the same, but the direction is completely different and looks alien to me.

It is the same velvet, the same rose, but its outlook is different. You can now put it back in its usual position and know that its intention is just the same, i.e. to help you to focus. Think of it as you having new spectacles. You see the same things *through* them, but you see better and clearer – and this you will do. Trust Me and trust your machine. You have absorbed more than you realise already.

When you write a letter it is not the writing that matters, but what you are saying. It is necessary for the recipient to be able to read your writing, but more important to be able to understand the message.

When you post that letter you entrust it to others to deliver it, to take care of it. You really do not need to know whether it is going by air, sea or train, so long as it gets to its destination.

So with your writing. It is important it reaches its useful destination in the best form to forward it. All those dealing with this work will be guided by Me to do what is best. You have already done the work, done it further than putting it down. You have 'seen' it reaching those who will benefit by its 'news'. Of course, they already know what is in it, but they forget to remember and we, you and I, are jogging their memories and helping them to overcome Fear, to enjoy Life, to Help your world.

Do not lose sight of the end product by concentrating too much on the part that will not be yours to operate. The set-up is already in place and just has to be organised in an on-going way. You do not start your car in top gear, you go through the gears to experience a smooth ride.

What about feedback?

Yes, you will get feed-back and by then you will be experienced enough with your tools to deal with it.

Trust Me, remember?

STARVATION

Dear God, it seems so long since I tuned-in seriously; I start doubting I might lose the link. What questions shall I ask? A friend wonders why the homeless and starving in India and Africa continue to have babies when they cannot feed those they already have?

Their instinct is to put down roots, to continue their tribes. All cultures have this wish to continue their line, be it a family or a nation.

What has caused the situation they are in? Is it not 'civilised' man's interference with nature? The weather patterns have been distorted, the forests have been decimated. Crops from the lands of the coloured races have been 'stolen' by white people who have paid poor prices to those who know not how to trade. Greed again. Even small children are made to work; there is slave labour still going on in this twenty-first century.

Your education systems have not taught truth and honesty; not emphasised the need for good thought, kindness to your brothers. All is done for gain. Yes, even those of you who consider yourselves honest and fair often ignore the well-being of those around you. You speed in your cars through populated areas regardless of the danger you may cause.

You have more clothes and food than you require, but how many of you give away your surplus? The starving have nothing to give away, yet they do not desert their children nor cry out in anger. Where is pity and thoughtfulness? Would the Master Jesus have ignored these people? You are so slow to learn.

The starving need resources for building themselves homes, sowing crops, living a life. They need self-respect. A child does not learn by having everything done for it, but by being shown how to do things for itself, to feed itself, to look after itself.

Isn't a great deal being done for these people in the way of relief work, volunteers, money for water supplies, etc.?

Yes, but it is a drop in the ocean. So much time is spent on what you call 'red tape' and so much paper is wasted on administration. If you were all the honest people you like to think you are there would be no need for this double digging.

You are being quite judgmental today!

I am stating facts. Facts are not judgmental. Facts are facts. If I do your learning and remembering for you, how will that help you? If you all start telling each other how perfect you are, where will that get you? Yet I tell you, you are perfect and I see you as that, but I also see how you have lost your way, how you waste your resources, forget to show compassion, forget that you are Spiritual Beings.

There is hope, there is Light ahead. Look for it and join in it. Know the Truth and the Truth shall make you free. Remember? Seek for knowledge, knock on the door for entry and you will find ways to receive, then give help to others. And this applies not only to helping the starving and homeless, but to the putting into practice of healthier ways of living, cleaner transportation, better communication one with another. Be Love. Know fulfilment. Love one another.

DOOM & GLOOM

11.5.02

The weather is cold and grey; the news is all doom and gloom; there has been another rail crash in this country; it is difficult to be cheerful and optimistic. Where is there progress, dear God?

Dear Child, I am with you. When you can laugh at your own mistakes, as you did today, through your temporary incompetence with your new computer, and the ensuing results, you can keep on the path of positivity and sanity. All is not doom and gloom as it appears to you. I have told you before, much is being achieved that you do not know of.

164

All those of you who read these words, pray for Peace, pray for enlightenment, pray for brotherly love.

You long to be well and happy. Some of you do not realise that deep down you long for these things. You let negativity take hold. You worry – and when you think about it what does that achieve?

Keep affirming the Truth – All is Well Now. You cannot get off the wheel of eternity. But you can revolve with it all the time. You can look on with ever more understanding. Try to enter the souls of those who are suffering, to feel their sorrow and fear; to understand their mistrust of their fellow beings. Then pray for their enlightenment; pray for their strength and understanding; for their development of peace in their hearts.

We are talking about the warring peoples; those who think gain of possessions is the be-all and the end-all. They cannot see that their violence is holding them back.

Pray for Peace over all your earth plane. See Peace, Be Peace, Act Peace, starting in your homes and in your work place, in your communities, in your own countries, then see it spreading out to all Lands. Picture Perfect Love pouring down upon all peoples, wherever they may be. Use your powerful imagination, your understanding, your love, your deepest feelings to spread out like a great cloak. Be part of that cloak. Wrap it around your fellow beings, including your animals.

Then see the destruction of all armaments, all weapons of destruction, all Feelings of Anger, All hatred, All Fear, Dissolve it in the glow of Love. You can do so much with your thoughts. I keep telling you this, but you are slow to learn and to put my words into practice. Open up a channel, each one of you, by focusing on a ray of pure golden light descending from heaven onto your earth plane. It is Great, it is Mighty, it IS REAL. Use it. It is greater than the air, the sunshine, that are always there. Use your power for peace. You are so powerful, my children, Use your Power. Love your neighbours. Start with your immediate neighbours, your countrymen, then all other countries. Do not judge. Be strong and know that I am guiding you, pushing you, into Peace. Your world is so beautiful, but you have forgotten how to use your Mind.

I do not condemn nor punish you. You do that to yourselves. I give you Love at all times.

Nothing, no thing, can harm the real you. When you are fearful just call my name in whatever language. I am always with you and all fear will drop away, even in the face of death. There is no death; just a moving from one level to another. There is no space, no time, no separation. You cannot stop or eradicate a beam of sunshine from descending on your earth. You can obscure it with buildings, you can run into what seems like shade, but that ray is always there. You are always in it and it is in you. Cherish it, glory in it, bathe in it, know you are part of it and cannot be separated. Then use that ray over all. It is strengthening; it is full of all goodness, all nourishment; use it in all that you do, whether it be working in the fields, working in your garden, making your meals, nursing your child or your fellow man. Use that ray for it is My Light, My Love, My Essence. My Being. It blesses you my dear ones.

EUTHANASIA

15.5.02

Will you tell us about the trauma Diane Pretty had to endure. Why did she have to suffer so long with motor neurone disease even when she chose to die, had no fear of death and those around her wished her suffering to cease?

This is an instance when you think you are not going to receive a satisfactory answer, isn't it?

Yes, because I know how I feel about it and what I would want.

There are rules and regulations in all countries and amongst all tribes and religions. They are man-made. When man makes them he thinks they are what is best for the people, usually to keep law and order, peace and fairness.

Why are these rules necessary? Because mainly they are for the protection of the individual against harm. However, sometimes they are taken to such lengths and become so complicated that you need lawyers to sort them out, often to add to them or to alter them.

When you are more understanding and more advanced you will not require so much discipline. When you learn to do without money there will be a vast change in many, many directions.

Now I am not being unnecessarily facetious here. When your dog or cat or other pet is very poorly, suffering great pain, you feel right, not happy, to have it 'put down' as you call it. You grieve for it, but you have done what you think was right at the time. Now that animal has no possessions

166

of its own, its kennel or basket or plate is of no value to anyone else or to the animal's relations.

When humans die, they leave possessions. These are of value, sometimes of great value, and involve your old curse, Money. Those left behind who are materialistic, often grasping, gimme, gimme types, squabble over what they think should be theirs.

We have talked about not being satisfied with your space and wanting other people's lands and countries and how that causes wars. In the case of the deceased it causes greed or possessiveness to take over.

There is no death and you cannot take your earthly possessions with you. Nor will you miss them.

As there is no death, as Life is eternal, it does not matter when you change coats. Those who do not believe this feel duty bound to keep you earth-bound and to see that no one else inherits your worldly goods without absolute clarity of intent.

To prevent murders and manslaughter you make laws. In a case like Diane's, your judges and magistrates are afraid to alter the law, or make exceptions, however much wiser it seems, because it will, or might, cause premature deaths. So you impose your laws because you are AFRAID of the consequences in other cases. It comes back to money.

How happy do possessions and money make you? Do you think purloining another's possessions can make you nearly as happy as awakening into a perfect world, where you have all you need, every beauty, all you desire, not to mention loss of pain, gain of perfect health.

Money, Fear, Death are poor substitutes for compassion, Love, understanding, selflessness, the realisation of eternal life.

The answer is in your hands. You have free choice, but sometimes, when you need to use it most, you are not allowed to by your fellow human beings.

Recall that there are those who know when their time has come to leave this world, and they walk up into the hills, lie down and leave their worn out garment on the hillside. These are those you often call primitive!

WORKAHOLICS

Would you tell me why some of us are workaholics; why we take on more than we can comfortably manage to do; why we push ourselves further than our commonsense tells us to go?

You are all the same and you are all different. Some are slow, some are quick; some are pessimistic, some are optimistic; some are lazy, some are hardworking.

Now you give yourselves these names, these descriptions. You know the saying, 'all things in moderation, including moderation'.

You think you know well your fellow man, yet you do not know how he or she feels inside. You cannot feel what another is feeling, experiencing. You think you can, but this is where you should not judge. You think I will tell you which attitudes are better, but by now you know I will only tell you there is no right and wrong!

My Dear Ones, you are all learning and some of you learn the hard way. You can 'lose out', as you call it, by being too slow and you can lose out by being too fast. You can be indifferent to another's plight, or you can be too sympathetic, thus giving away your own strength in your endeavour to help.

There is the 'happy medium' in all things. If you will remember that all is perfect, all is peace and calm, there is no time nor space, there is enough of everything for everyone, then it is easier for you to strike the right note, which is right in the centre. Does this answer your question?

Sometimes it is so difficult to change because our whole being seems geared up or geared down to be as we are.

Which is the smoother run, if we are talking about gears? Too slow and you hold up others, too fast and the ride is bumpy and dangerous for yourself and your passengers. There is the comfortable speed, the comfortable temperature, the best way to be for the sake of those around you.

Who are the people you most like being with? In whose company are you most comfortable, most relaxed? Think about this and each one can find their own answer.

FREE CHOICE

We have talked before about there being no Coincidence or Chance and I passionately believe this. Looking back on my own life convinces me of this, yet sometimes I have a problem with where Free Choice comes in.

I could decide now to shut down my computer and drive to the nearest town for a specific reason, and that would be my Free Choice. Then supposing I had a bad accident on my journey – that would not be a coincidence, there would be some reason for it – so where did my Free Choice lead me?

Just before you tuned-in to Me, you telephoned to see if a friend was at home as you wished to deliver a gift to her. There was no reply, so you will never know if that saved you from an accident during that journey!

So in a way, we haven't Free Choice, because what you have just said makes me think we are always being guided in the way that is best for us at that moment in time.

Guidance is always there for you, but you have free choice as to whether you listen to it. Sometimes you talk about using, or not using, 'your better judgment'.

We also talk about 'taking a chance' – that really seems to mix up choice, chance and coincidence! I feel confused here.

You are making choices during most of your waking hours and mostly they are not of great consequence, either to yourself or to others. Your time factor comes in to many of them. It is the big choices you make or the big chances you take, that involve many others, where your free choice really matters.

Big Business, Wars, Laws, that is where the free choice of the few can affect the many. The consequences can be great and do not happen by chance or coincidence. This is where your great friend and power, Prayer, can come in. Prayer for Good for All will bring Good for All. Prayer for revenge would not be prayer. Your Power is in prayer for Peace and Love.

I am not a person. I am your Higher Self, your Wisdom, your true Love, your Spirit – one with another because we are all One. Love Me and you love yourself; love yourself and you love your neighbour as yourself. Love one another my children.

GUILT & REMORSE

Do we sometimes feel guilty when there is no need? I ask this in order to guide me in trying to help two friends who feel guilty.

Listen to your innermost, your conscience, your inner knowing. Ask yourself questions. Why do you feel guilty? Why did you do or say what you did?

You now have hindsight, but at the time of a happening did you do what you felt was best in that situation? If you did what you did or said out of spite or revenge or temper you will, if you have now progressed on your path, feel uncomfortable with yourself. If, after deep thought, you feel justified in what you did or said, then you would probably act the same way again.

What is done is done.

Should one feel remorse?

Remorse, like worry, gets you nowhere, unless you learn from it. When you cannot alter some happening, let it go. If thinking about it can teach you a lesson, then think about it, but do not dwell on it. Remember about moderation in all things.

You all need to listen to yourselves as well as to others. Your tongue is a dangerous weapon, to be used with great care and caution. It is easier to forget a smite than an insult, a slap than a slight, a knock than an injustice.

There is no need to feel guilty over an action that has stopped quarrelling or caused peace. You have only two cheeks to turn.

On a worldwide scale, much is done in haste out of fear, without enough thought. Your prayers for Peace help to hinder unwise decisions. Halt before you pull the trigger; hesitate before you cast blame; think deeply about consequences. See where right action has brought good results instead of disaster.

Remember, you are never alone, whether you are a woman in the street or a prime minister leading a nation. Help and guidance are always with you – but you need to listen.

INSPIRATION

Having no idea what I was going to ask, I pictured my beautiful pink rose bud for guidance. From its reclining position it is resting its head on one 'hand' while turning the pages of a book with the other. Is that an indication that I must seek some new reading matter, I ask myself?

No, the book is then closed to show the title. In the past, when I have seen books, the print has never been legible, but not so today. The title is "GOOD GOD" in large gold lettering.

This is quietly exciting. I always wanted this work to be in book form. Then, when I had no luck with publishers, putting it out on the Internet seemed to be the way.

Can I now hope for both forms of communication?

May I remind you that all things are possible with God? And may I remind you to 'see' the finished article, then picture the process of editing and printing, then imagine the 'work' itself being done?

We have talked about this reverse order before, both in Neale's work and in yours. Imagery has great power, Thought has great power, making a Reality of something has great power. And these messages have great Power to reach and help and guide those who are ready to listen and act upon them.

When you open the door of a hive, many bees come out; when you open the door of a library many people go in, to see what they can find. All is movement; all is progress; all is planned.

When flooding commences water seeps through many places, from a trickle to a rush. So it is with knowledge. Mostly my people are curious; mostly they learn more than they anticipated.

You could add to your daily prayer list, a plea in the form of Light, that more and more people will seek out the Truth, absorb it and put it into practice.

GOD – ALL-KNOWING

I was feeling guilty for not having tuned-in for so long. Never have I sought more than one session in a day. Now I am communicating for a third time. Am I making up for lost time?

No, there is no time for this work. You are finding that your feeling of guilt was unnecessary. You have free will. I do not punish. I do not leave you, even when you think you have left me. Earlier today we talked about guilt. Has your lapse caused any hurt? Have I been out of your Mind? Have you lost your ability to tune-in?

The answer to these questions is 'No'. You let your old enemy, Fear, creep in with the guilt. Has that done any good? No, you have just stood still. Nothing has been lost. In fact you have just achieved a new skill with your computer by pushing away a bit of fear over some editing.

How do you know all this, my every move, my every thought, my every feeling? It could be quite scary, but it isn't. It is wonderful!

You know the answer. We are One, I am you and you are Me. I know the thoughts of all of you and, when you are on a higher plane, you know that speech will be unnecessary because you too will read each other's thoughts.

So we couldn't keep a secret or give a surprise?

Why would you want to? All is instantaneous, unconditional Love. The surprise is in experiencing it. The joy is in discovering it. Trust me.

ERRANT CHILDREN

It is alarming to witness how children are misbehaving in many of our towns all over our country. Mere children are causing adults to fear. You have said it is wrong to treat them in a similar way, that two wrongs do not make a right, but what is the solution? We need help and guidance to alter their outlook. What is wrong with them?

Usually I tell you there is no wrong and right, but in this case I am going to ask you if you do not think you, the adults, are at fault? Where do children learn to behave as they do? Is it not from the example you set them? Do you find children from loving, caring homes behaving like criminals?

While you show your children violence both in the home and on your television screens, can you wonder that they grow up to think that is the normal way to live?

How many homes do you know where all is peace, love, kindness, thoughtfulness? I have said elsewhere, training and example commence at birth, first with love, then with discipline.

But how do we teach the parents to be an example for good? They appear to thrive on quarrelling, shouting, abuse. It seems a horrendous task to tackle because most of them don't seem to mind how their children behave.

What has happened to ideals, example, standards, obedience and respect? Were these things taught to the parents? *They* need education before they can educate, example before they can be an example.

How many stories on your screens portray a happy, fulfilling way of life? You ask what you can do. You need to start at the source and work down. How much is done in the name of love? This applies from the top down, from your leaders, your preachers, your teachers, your elders, your relatives, your local government.

It could take years to alter these things. Meantime the mayhem goes on. The police have lost control, the prisons are overcrowded. You say we should not use force or corporal punishment. It is wrong of me, but I should like to see the parents being beaten up, deprived, frightened by each other, except I don't know what would happen to the kids while the parents were being persecuted.

You know in your heart that is not the answer. Two wrongs never did and never will make a right. You send missionaries abroad to teach the homeless and starving how to make a living, what to do with their lives, yet you cannot put your own country to rights. What has happened to your priorities? Example is all important. What examples are your setting?

What can we do about drugs?

Use your television screens and your schools to portray the consequences of drug-taking. Let addicts and ex-addicts tell their miserable stories, let them talk freely about their misery and its repercussions on others. Raise the expected standard of living, in the home, on the street, on public transport.

173

Who is going to pay for all this?

We are back on the old curse of money. Where does the money come from for your weapons of destruction? Where do the youngsters get their money to buy drugs? Your weapons steal lives, your youngsters steal from you and shops, anywhere, without thought for others. Not much thought is being given to others is it?

Would a return to National Service help?

Not if you really give deep thought to it. That teaches discipline, but it also teaches combat, fighting, war, the use of weapons. These are the very things you wish to obliterate, are they not?

Yes, but I cannot see a solution without using force, imprisonment, even violence. I find it most depressing, because it is getting worse and worse.

How do you train your animals, your plants, your apprentices? With kindness, persuasion, patience. You reward your animals with titbits, your plants with nutrition and twine, your apprentices with a little praise. Are you feeding these things to your children? Do they feel loved, cared for and rewarded for thoughtfulness. Think how you feel when you experience the care of another and how you feel when you give care to another.

You have forgotten how to be happy and how to make others happy. You say the world is a hard place, but who has made it seem that way? Do you really think you have your priorities right? You all need to experience love, discipline and self-love, then you can experience giving love, giving wisdom, giving selfless love. You have a song called "the best things in life are free". It is true and you need to experience it to believe it.

PERSONAL RESPONSIBILITY

World conditions seem to get worse by the day. Our weather is not predictable as much as it used to be, there is unrest and terrorism all over the world, Western economy is unstable, health conditions deteriorate in every country, mainly because of AIDS. Is all this our fault?

You have become satisfied with less than the best. Your standards have dropped. Simple delights are enjoyed by the few instead of the many. Greed and speed and noise give you false pleasure. You are so busy Doing. What has happened to Being? Do you stop to breathe in the fresh air in the countryside, or watch a small child at play? How much desire do you have to learn? Do you stop to be thankful for the roof over your head, the food in your body, the care of those who care for you? Do you ever bless the man who collects your rubbish or those who repair your street lighting? Do you really earn what you are paid?

Yes, many of you do use your goodness, your spiritual attributes, but many of you never give a thought to all that is around you, not deep thought.

Are you being judgmental?

I am stating facts. Sometimes facts are unpleasant. Sometimes facts are hard to grasp. Sometimes facts need understanding. Some go through their earth life without much thought for others, nor even thought for themselves and how they treat their bodies. You have been given a perfect piece of 'machinery' and it needs care and attention in great detail. It needs right food, right exercise, right maintenance.

Now in the 'engine' is a soul, an energy, something that makes it go. You cannot see it, but you know it is there and you know when it is not firing on all cylinders. Instead of ignoring the signs, it needs attention. Some of this maintenance is material, but the important part of the treatment is the energy field. The energy is all around you, in equal measure for all. There are no spaces in that energy, no flaws, it is all-knowing, all Truth. It is there for all of you to tune into and to use.

Yes, it is Me, whom you call God because you think of me as a person. I tell you, you are part of me and I am part of you. We are One. You cannot get away from me. Some of you have been taught, falsely, to fear me, to think I use retribution. It is you who punish yourselves. You use the wrong engine oil, you read the wrong manuals for your type of engine. You use the wrong tools. You do not need money or great knowledge to fine-tune your engine. I am there, watching your every move, your every thought. Learn to listen. My voice is quiet but it is strong. My language is simple but it is profound.

Why do you not try using Me? There is nothing, no thing, to stop you, only your own doubt, your own misgiving. Your pain is self-inflicted. I am talking about your mental pain, your psychological pain. There is so much truth in knowing 'Know the Truth and the Truth shall make you Free'.

Dear Ones, you are loved. Who ever you are, where ever you are, you are loved. Whether you are a little child, a woman in labour or an old man near death, you are all loved equally.

175

And that brings us to your fear of death. Why do you fear the inevitable? You know there is only one thing certain when you are born – you will die. Birth into your earth world is much more painful than birth back into the world you came from. The latter happens in the twinkling of an eye. Be prepared for your death by just putting a thought in the back of you head that one day you will have a wondrous experience. When that happens you will wish so much that you had told those you left behind what a wonderful experience you have just had!

All that you seem to suffer now is man-made. All could be put right by using that energy, that soul, that controls your engine. That is when you will experience heaven on earth. There are some who now experience that, though you might not think so by looking on at their simple lives, their lack of worldly goods, their simple outlook.

You really do not have to change very much to experience all this. Be satisfied with your engine, whether it is in a Mercedes or a Mini. Yes, I know all about your cars, after all I guided you to design them! Then think about the energy that runs them. Either can have a breakdown. And what causes that? Why, a part has gone wrong, has misfired, has ill-functioned, usually through your own error in lack of thought or maintenance. You take your problem to someone who is a mechanic, a specialist in that field, or you use your own knowledge. There is a short cut with your bodily engine – you can come straight to me. Bring me your problems. I already know what is going wrong, but I cannot help you if you do not wish for my advice.

I, too, have a Degree in mending bodies and souls. I invite you to use me and there is no charge, everyone can afford my advice and it is given with nothing but Love, because I designed you in the first place and deep within you know that.

SPIRIT GUIDES

Oh dear. Can I ask questions about which I know nothing? I have just received a list, which you will know about, dear God.

You cannot learn French in the middle of a Maths lesson. You do not use Maths during a history lesson, well, only very loosely. The questioner is on a different wavelength with most of what she has asked.

176

As to spirit guides being parts of yourselves – yes, because we are all One. You may feel familiar with your guide because of past relationship or contact, or, what you feel may be because that guide has chosen to be with you during your earth life, giving you tremendous love, protection and guidance. Try to imagine the number of aspects of the Whole you have experienced during many, many incarnations.

We have talked about the 'work you choose to do' on the next plane of your Being and how you may choose to become a guide. There are many reasons why you might choose to be a guide and it is not always personal. You may choose to guide those who are working on something that particularly interests you. Having learned more about that interest, you then wish to pass that knowledge on, to guide, another or others still working on your earth plane.

You forget to remember that you have experienced, or will experience, all things. You have known what it is like to be an insect, an animal, a flower, a tree.

What about the experience of being a great wave, an earthquake, a storm?

That is the experience of great power. With your present knowledge you cannot feel so much power per se, you can fear it, you can try to imagine it; you would not know how to use it. Recall how poorly you use the power that you now have. You use it for destruction of others. You use it to cause fear in others, be they human beings or animals and birds.

I have told you, you are very little children, still in the junior schools.

As to magnetic forces, floods, climatic conditions, mankind has to learn (remember) how to treat the earth plane. He forgets to pour out love and compassion to all creatures, all plant life, the very earth itself. You are making haste so slowly. Just when a seemingly new discovery is found, someone else often smashes it with negativity.

May I suggest you, yourself, stop feeling so inadequate – you are swimming against the tide! You will feel more at peace when you next tune-in – I promise you.

UNEXPECTED LOVE

It is wonderful to experience Love. I am not talking about the beautiful love from our families and great friends. I am talking about the unexpected love from acquaintances and even strangers. I have been greatly privileged to feel this love, especially in the last few weeks. Would you explain how we can all come to know this feeling.

This is a two-way experience, my children. It is a progression, a giving and a taking.

You are always surrounded by Love. You need to become conscious of it and to use it at every opportunity. Be more ready to expand yourselves, to fill yourselves with this Love, then to push, yes push, it out. You see for yourselves how animals and birds respond to love. When they feel it from you they take a step towards you instead of away from you.

So with people. Your consciousness thrives on love. You feel it upon you, like the warmth of the sun. Imagine having a special Day when all people agreed to give out love, to everyone and to everything. You would smile at everyone and make eye contact with everyone and you would be glowing.

Now imagine doing that every day of your life! What is there to stop you? Who is stopping you? Why you, yourselves, are afraid to 'come out of your shells', to show your feelings. Suddenly there would be heaven on earth.

Some of you are beginning to experience this. Love touches Love and it makes you want to explode with happiness. Such simple little acts or words can start a chain reaction. It is very infectious and knows no boundaries. It reaches across all barriers, from the garden fence to another continent. You do not realise this is what you are trying to do, to create, to experience.

If you think this is not possible, try shutting out the sun from your surroundings on a sunny day. You can shut your eyes, but as soon as you open them the sun is there. So it is with Love – it is there. Grasp it, give it away, treasure it, scatter it. Every cell of your body, every thought in your mind, would be conscious of it.

Why are celebrations usually so enjoyable for most people? Because they are celebrations of love, an expression of love one to another. Sometimes they are celebrations of thankfulness, for a life or a life together, or an achievement. You can celebrate with champagne or with sparkling water from a mountain stream, perhaps just celebrating the beauty of your surroundings.

You talk about an atmosphere. You can be uplifted by atmosphere and the strongest atmosphere is one of Love. Remember Love is another word for Life. There are just as heartfelt tears of joy as of sorrow. You experience a 'letting out' of such wonderful feelings that you cannot contain them within yourselves and you even shout for joy.

Whatever your life appears to be, try celebrating each day with love and joy – another day, another experience, another celebration, be it minute or tremendous. Love one another.

DISCERNMENT

Dear God, at this moment in time I could give way to slight depression, but I Choose not to. The summer weather we long for came and went in a few days and was so extremely hot and humid it was difficult to keep going; now it is wet, dull and cold. Will we ever get back the predictable weather when we knew what to expect from the seasons in this part of the world?

Be still and know that I am God. I am not a person, not a demanding entity to fear, not aloof and far away. I am in you and you are in me. I know your thoughts, your feelings, your fears.

Remember to be responsible for I make no demands upon you. You choose your earthly rulers, then you either obey them or condemn them. You give them power, you praise them, you criticise them. You choose your laws, your rules, your standards. How much deep thought, good thought, God thought, goes into all these choices?

You have free will. You have free choice; you have whatever freedom you make for yourselves.

You do not realise or believe that you are so powerful. You say, 'Why does God let this or that happen? How can a loving God allow such things? Why doesn't God step in and make things better, make people more thoughtful?'

My dear ones, would you then have free will? No of course not – you would be doing My will.

Do you think if you asked for my help and guidance in all you do, think and say, there would be an improvement?

179

Many of you deny my existence. You scoff in a superior way at the simple souls who follow a simple path. Some of you refuse to believe that there is much in your holy books that is false; that it is man-written.

Read with the Truth that is within you. In you is all Truth. It is deep beneath the trivial, arrogant, seemingly intellectual thoughts that run through your minds. As I have said before, it is your conscience – your consciousness of divine Truth which your conscience is – that you need to use. I am always there, you cannot get rid of me, but you can deny me. You forget that I love you more than anyone else loves you. I AM the real you.

Pray for guidance, pray to reach that Truth within you. Reach deep within when you speak, when you act, when you feel the need to feel Love.

As you use Me your life will seem easier; ways will open up to you; knowledge will come to you; true friends will cross your path; all things will be made new; your Truth will set you free.

You cannot know normality if you do not experience abnormality. You cannot appreciate comfort if you do not experience discomfort. You cannot appreciate your comfort zone if you do not experience extremes of heat and cold. You cannot appreciate the love of others, even strangers, if you have not experienced the wrath or cruelty of those you love.

Be grateful for your seeming troubles, for without them your life would be bland, uneventful. In some ways you like the ups and downs, the sorrows, yes even the sorrows, and the great joys, the tears and the laughter. Every one of your days is a challenge, a test, an experience. At the end of each day you can be wiser.

Feel loved, even amidst the turmoil, illness, hardship, for you are never not loved. I am always there to guide and show you the way. Use me at all times, in all circumstances. You cannot shock me, you cannot repulse me for I am ALWAYS there, right with you.

Think before you speak, think before you act, think before you condemn, think before you judge and think before you love; yes, before you love, because when you truly love you give without measure, without doubt, without any limitations. Love is All.

Oh, how different the world would be if we lived in this way. What fools we are to give so little thought to how we live and think. You mentioned temperatures, but you did not indicate if climatic conditions would revert to their former patterns.

All is movement. You can read elsewhere what mankind has done to the earth's climate and atmosphere. In your hearts, your innermost, (that we have just been talking about), you know what is happening and why. You are realising about pollution. You are experiencing results you do not like. The paths to the future are your choice. I can, of course, light the best routes!

OPEN-MINDEDNESS

When I say to people, "Of course there is no death; we are going somewhere lovely", often adding, " We are going back to where we came from", the general response is, "There is no proof." Men especially are as dogmatic as I am. I sometimes add, "You know all this in your heart centre," pointing to it. What proof is there, except that inner knowing? For myself, I cannot ever remember doubting it, having to learn or remember it. Admittedly I have learned a great deal more about our eternal life through study and reading, but I so wish to convince others.

If your dog or your small child will not cross a stream to get to the other side, you carry it. Explaining there is more land to land on is no use. They do not understand; they are afraid.

The people you speak of are afraid to believe, though they would most likely not admit to it being a fear. They do not want to think about an ending to their present existence. Life for them is simpler the way they think. They do not need proof at the moment you are speaking to them. You may even be upsetting their level.

For those who really wish, or Choose, to know more, of course there is proof. There are thousands of books, including your Bible, that give proof. There are genuine Mediums that will tune-in to those 'on the other side' and give them proof by telling them some incident that no one else could know.

You, you, you, all of you have Free Choice. You can remain still or you can go ahead, like crossing the stream. Either you can go alone (as you think you are, but are not!) or you can choose to go with the help of another. You can wake up that heart centre to learn more about any subject you wish. You, yourself, would not choose to learn more about electricity or economics, you leave that to others, but there is nothing to stop you.

You think how sad it is that there are those who think this earth life is the All. But does it matter? A scientist might feel sorry for you, not wanting to know more about science, but as you are not trying to solve something that needs that knowledge, it does not matter. Were you to be stranded in isolation, where it was vital you knew how to save yourself by understanding how to get out of a situation, you would make an effort and in doing so would be open to the promptings of your all-knowledge, suggesting to you what to do.

Now if you knew beforehand that you were going to be in that position, you would think 'I had better learn a bit about this so that I can get out of that situation' and you could do so. Likewise if you were told you had only so long to remain in your earth body, you would quite likely start wanting to know, or remember, what was coming next, if anything. Or, if a loved one was in that position you might want to comfort them with hope, or yourself with the hope that you would not be parted for good. This would be another good reason for doing a little study. And it is surprising to those people how the 'right' people turn up in their lives to help them. You are inclined to forget that I play a large part here! I send others to you, or you to them and mostly you say, "What a coincidence, or, that was pure Chance." Well, I tell you, it is all arranged, it is already mapped out – all ready.

Your free choice is when you, YOU, are ready and willing to learn and remember more, that you find All is Ready. All Truth is already in your heart. You need have no fears that no one will be with you when your time of need or your time of 'wish' occurs. You let your small child try to walk on its own, but you are there ready to catch it. I am always there ready to catch you my beloved children.

WORLD PROGRESS

Dear God, why do I concern myself with what question I am going to ask you? There must be endless information and help you wish, at all times, to convey to us. We do not seem to be progressing in our way of living. In fact, the reverse appears to be happening.

There is progress, my child, but you are mostly unaware of it for it does not make 'news' as does the violence, the aggression, the horror stories.

Mostly you live in fear. There is fear of war, murder, pollution, accident, and all that on a general scale. There are homes where there is continual fear of aggression, bullying, abuse, sexual abuse, illness, thieving, quarrelling.

Do you consider any of this is My doing? Do you think I am causing any of this to happen?

It is all man's inhumanity to man. All these fears are caused by man. Where is Love? Where is love towards one another, towards your neighbour, your brother, your parents, your teachers? Love towards those to whom you give power? Where is unselfishness, care, consideration one for another?

And where would you learn these attributes? Why, firstly in the home, then at school, then in each section of life as you live through your earth incarnation.

Of course there is great compassion being shown in many of your institutions, but it mostly goes unnoticed. Some of your happiness and peace is taken, by those who experience it, for granted. There are those who at the end of the day thank me for their blessings. Thank yourselves also for you and I are One. We are all part of perfect Life, perfect Love. You experience ecstasy in 'drinking in' those moments of love, be it from your dog, your child, your partner, your mentor.

Your lives are in your hands. You often say, some of you, my life is in God's hands. Well it is, but you forget that you and I are one and we are both, and all, wanting Good.

How can I believe we are all wanting Good when I watch road rage, abduction, destruction, greed?

There is a great lack in the lives of those who adversely affect the lives of their brother man. They think you have something they have not; they want, want, want, what in fact they already have. And what is that? It is the things that are free for all of you. There is enough for all, be it land, food, goods, and above all – Love. A great need has been left out of their upbringing and, yes, that is love. You have a song that tells you 'the best things in life are free'. Of course they are, but how many people stop to realise that. All the money in the world will not buy you Love, Peace, Contentment. You do not even have to earn them. They are all there, free and in abundance. Yes, even for the homeless and starving because you do not share your resources.

We have talked elsewhere about not being satisfied with your patch.

Look back to your childhood. What are the happiest memories? Are they of occasions when a great deal of money was spent? Are they not of the occasion when your grandmother spent time showing you how to do or make something? When you played with favourite toys that seemed real animals or babies to you? When you felt Love and were given Time? And was a holiday great because of what you were doing or because of what you were Being – which was part of a family, your own or someone else's. Did you have a best friend because they were rich or because you felt a common bond of real friendship, common interests?

My dear Ones, your priorities have gone sadly awry. Do your pets have anything to give you except love, loyalty and companionship? How often do I have to say 'pray', 'think deeply', judge not, send out Love instead of criticism.

Give out Love, love from your heart centre. Pour love into that heart centre, not fear. Fear is an absence of understanding, a making of reality of something that does not really exist. There is no death, no ending, only a moving on. You want that move to be to a better place, an existence of peace and joy and it can be that now, this minute. Use your Power for Good which I have given you in abundance. You can send out good thoughts, peaceful thoughts, loving thoughts to all the world. As I have told you many, many times, your prayers are so powerful. You do not have to pray for yourselves, for you already have all you need. If you disagree with that, then pray that you may understand more fully.

If you move from A to B you will be no happier if you take your same thoughts and ideas with you. If you move back to A from B you will feel no different unless you take a different set of ideas and wisdom with you.

You cannot live apart from one another because you are all one. But you can alter your outlook, your motives, your feelings. If you want someone else to alter, then alter yourself, your thoughts, your idea of them. I see you all as my perfect creation. Have you created some of my children as less than perfect in your mortal mind? Rise above that critical, mortal mind.

You have just altered the direction of the air from your electric fan because you feel so hot. Has the fan changed? Has the air changed? No, you are accepting it from a different angle. You are letting a breeze cool you down. You are appreciating a more comfortable feeling. That, you think, is rather a silly thought, too simplistic. But Life is simple, solutions are already there, but you place barriers, objections, arguments in the way of the obvious. Yes, this is a simple statement, but it applies to many of man's actions. He makes simple things complicated. He wants too much,

184

too fast. Slow down, stop the stress, stop the need for speed; there is all the time in the world – and outside of your world, for time goes on for ever. It never runs out, so why the rush?

SOHAM

19.8.02

Dear God, will you please convey through me a message for the people of Soham and in particular for the parents and siblings of Holly and Jessica.

Be comforted in the sure knowledge that there is no death. Try to rise above the terrible trauma you are feeling at this time. Let go of the pain and grief that are overwhelming you. Go to your heart centre, the very centre of your Being where all Life, Love and Truth reside.

Be very still. Try to feel that Peace. Know that I am with you, with you all. I am God, Good, and you and I are one. You are part of Me and I am part of you. There is no separation. Feel that Oneness. You can do this, even if just for a moment. Hold that oneness.

Now know that those little girls are part of that Oneness, one with each other, one with all of you. There is No Death. They are happy and whole and complete. They are now on a different 'level'. They are not suffering and they do not want you to suffer. See their happy faces; they are telling you, 'We are fine, we are safe. We shall see you again. We now know there is no death. Try to feel us near you for we shall come near you whenever you call us and pray for us. It is true that we are All One'.

Dear Ones, be comforted. I, God, am with you at all times. You cannot get away from me, you cannot be separate. There is no space between us. You cannot now separate the love you are all giving out, one for another. You cannot cut it into pieces and put one piece here and one piece there. You cannot separate the Light that is all around you. You can place obstacles in its beam, but it is still there. You cannot separate Love or Good because you are part of them at all times.

When you doubt my words, go back into your heart centre where all Truth is. Comfort and love each other, feel that oneness. There are no strangers. You are all from the Source and you remain in it, then return to it at what you call your end, but there was no beginning and there is no end.

Save your ifs and buts for a later time, when you are not so sorrowful. The right people and the right books will come to you when you are ready for them.

185

It is difficult for you to believe at this time that nothing happens by chance. There are no coincidences. Be satisfied for the present to be as little children, accepting this Truth into your hearts. You are as little children. I am your Greater Intelligence, not a person. I am always with you, AT ALL TIMES.

You have free will to think and behave as You Choose. Choose now to grow in knowledge. Holly and Jessica are truly alive; they are surrounded by Love and they are not unhappy, for they have experienced the fact of Life Everlasting and they are Being that right now.

Be still and know the God, the Good, that is ever in your heart. Do not judge the cynics that try to tell you this is all airy, fairy nonsense. Be sorry for them for they have not yet learned your Truth. In fact you could think, 'Pray God that they do not have to learn their truth in this traumatic way'.

I am with you. I am with you. Say that many times, putting the emphasis on a different word each time, for you are declaring my Truth.

Your prayers are heard and you do not have to be in a certain place or a special position to say them. Just speak in your head wherever you are and whenever you wish. You will be comforted. You will be happy again. You will learn from this experience. You will have learned how to comfort each other and those still to come into your lives who will need comfort. When you know what pain feels like, you are better able to understand when others come to you in their pain.

Let Me into your hearts. Listen for my voice, feel my love. You will come to recognise it, then you will seek it more often. Do not fear for fear is destructive.

Be gentle with each other, especially with your little ones. And Children, be kind to each other. Sometimes those who are very quiet most need comfort and understanding.

My Love IS with you. Feel it, use it, wrap it around you – there is more than enough for all the world.

IRAQ

8.9.02

Oh, dear God, what a lot of Fear must be generating at this time with regard to Iraq. I keep holding the thought of Peace over all the world, particularly the troubled countries and their Leaders. We cannot help fearing war, especially with the knowledge of nuclear weapons and germ warfare. Please tell us again how best to keep Peace.

Picture the great Light of Peace and Love – a brilliant Light so bright you can scarcely look at it with your spiritual eye. Hold that Light over all your earth; see the earth revolving slowly in the Light. Hesitate over the countries that particularly need guidance, especially your own country and the United States.

Now hold the Leaders of all those countries in the Light. Concentrate on them, first individually, then together. Hold them together in the Light for you are all One.

Now hold that picture for as long as you can. Be in complete silence within, shut out any extraneous noise. See those Leaders as one with each other and with you all. You are All One.

Hold no hatred in your heart. Remember the peoples of all countries involved have the same fear as your own. They, too, fear for their families, their homes, their health, their well-being. They fear similar consequences that you do. In the hearts of all, beneath the fear, is a longing for peace. Remember those leaders, called presidents, prime ministers, chancellors, emperors, whatever, have only the earthly, mortal power that you, their people, have given them. Their power is as nothing compared with My Power. Then remember you and I are one, therefore you can beam them my Power.

Think deeply about this Light and Power. Try not to fear, for that is your worst enemy. True Power is Love and Love is true Power.

See Peace, Be Peace, live Peace. See Light, Be Light, live Light. See Love, Be Love, live Love. Peace, Light, Love, oh my dear ones, these three conditions are the Power. Use them. Keep using them. The more of you who practise this, the more Power for Good and Peace is being generated.

I am with you Always, All Ways.

LIFE EXPERIENCES

In Neale's Trilogy ("Conversations with God") you frequently say we are here to remember, not to learn. This would indicate that we have already experienced everything before, yet surely we live through new experiences in every incarnation to teach us to progress? If not, what is the point of reincarnation?

Your answer lies in the fact of how you responded to those experiences. You can look at a picture many times before you really see it and what it portrays. You can read a deep book several times before you really understand its message. You can fall in the sea and not know how to swim. You can cause trouble in your family or your work place without knowing why you do it.

You have a saying 'it is not what you know, but who you know'. What we are talking about is how you re-acted to past experiences. So, yes, you are here to remember past experiences within your soul and use your more awakened knowledge to deal with similar experiences now.

Give me an easy example.

Let us say that many centuries ago (in your idea of time) you were cruel to your children. You had the same knowledge of right and wrong, the same conscience, that you all have now.

I must interrupt, because you say there is no right and wrong.

Let us say, you had the same choice of how to treat your children, the same choice that you have now. You had free will.

At that time you did not listen to your inner knowing, you gave way to temper, impatience, thoughtlessness. You caused others to suffer. You caused others to feel hate, injustice, fear. Meanwhile you were unable to experience joy, love, unselfishness, peace, for yourself. So there are now many things that require putting right, both for yourself and for others.

Strangely, you may think, you were an example to others by which they could benefit. They could see what not to be like, how not to behave, and very importantly you taught them compassion and forgiveness. You, yourself, eventually felt remorse, disappointment, shame, guilt. And according to what your religion had taught you, probably great Fear. You started wondering about punishment, everlasting damnation, hell.

What a long list of problems you caused, both to others and to yourself. At the finish of that incarnation you had changed little. But you may have done some good! You know how? You may have taught some people never to be like that and to put into practice love and forgiveness.

When you chose to reincarnate you also chose to meet up with some of those you had bruised. You had a great desire to love them. You had a desire to experience all that in your soul, you knew to be beautiful.

This conversation we are having gives you all much food for thought. Think about your present life. Recall all that has occurred – and your re-actions to situations. If you feel very loved, begin to realise you have earned that joy; if you feel deserted and unloved begin to wonder why. How do you behave now? How much love do you give out? How much self-righteousness do you feel? How much criticism do you hold? Only you know, and I, the Real You.

If you DO to Get, if you GIVE to Get, if you LOVE to Receive, how much are those acts worth?

If you DO to Give pleasure and love, if you GIVE to give thanks, if you LOVE without expectation, how much are those acts worth?

You do not know at what stage of remembering your fellow beings are. Remembering that, helps you to be compassionate, understanding, forgiving, loving. Using this knowledge, remembering your original state of perfection, helps you to experience joy, peace, love and, yes, ecstasy.

FEELINGS

Why do we have days when we feel 'on top of the world' and others when we feel depression? I am asking about ordinary days, not ones that would naturally cause those ups and downs.

There are many reasons for these moods, these feelings.

Again, choice comes into this. You can choose what piece of music you will play or listen to, what book or article you will read, which friend you will contact, whether you will stay at home or go out; will you occupy yourself with some job, or make a journey? Will you let the weather affect your feelings?

Will you dwell on the negative side of a situation or spend time working out a solution?

According to your choices, so will your mood vary.

Let us use some examples. Suppose you have let someone you care about, ruffle your feathers, as you say. Will you dwell on this, feel hard done by, suffer injustice, even feel resentment? All these thoughts have already passed through your mind. Will you recall them and keep passing them through or will you let go of them?

When you let go of them you can, seemingly, leave an empty space. Better than that is to rise above that negativity. Feel sorry for the person who has let another person or situation 'get to them'. Instead of extending the chain, refuse to be another link. Give the situation the thought, that the perpetrator forgot to give the situation. Instead of a mole hill having turned into a mountain, let it go back to that little mole hill.

Sometimes thoughts have been voiced and the tongue has caused much damage. Refuse to let your own tongue cause more damage, usually making a situation worse. There are so many sayings that apply here: pour oil on troubled waters, turn the other cheek, hear all, see all and say nought. Sit quietly and add all the positivity you can. Remember how powerful your thoughts are. Either let a situation solve itself, or put positive thinking into action or bury any feelings of hurt or revenge that you are feeling. If this someone we are speaking of cares for you as you care for them, they will not wish to fall out with you, or if they were voicing their feelings about another, help them with wise counsel, explaining the situation from another angle.

Sometimes we need to let others learn their own lessons; in a case like that just keep quiet. Again your sayings come into play: less said soonest mended; hold your tongue; keep the peace.

Perhaps your mood is caused because there is something ahead that you do not want to face? If the situation has to be faced anyway, face it, knowing that you will get the other side of it. Whatever comes to you to deal with, do it with love. Yes, even when you think 'where is there love here?' What you are doing each day, either in thought or physically, monetarily, verbally, manually, do it with love for there is an end result. Someone or something is going to benefit, be it your garden, your friend, your supplier, your employer or employee. Even supposing you have to dismiss an employee, know that it can benefit them eventually, so long as you do it with love.

Do you recall how Louise Hay often kisses her cheques as she sends them, because she remembers she is paying for a service that she has been grateful to receive.

Yes, it really does help to remember that, when paying the gas bill or the Income Tax! After all, we needed the gas, and without the tax there would be no money to pay for necessary government expenses such as schools, hospitals, utilities, etc.

As to the good days, most life responds to sunshine. You see the flowers opening, the animals sunning themselves, the people enjoying themselves. Then what about cheery words? A smile? The sound of laughter? Each of you can help to lift the mood of another. You can look for happiness just as some of you look for trouble!

Whatever your feelings or your problems you can always tune-in to Me. Then when you truly listen you will hear. It is also good to tune-in with your joys and your thankfulness and your happiness. Do you know why? Because it makes you more conscious of it!

MONEY

God, I am having a problem about money. You refer to it in some of my conversations with you as being a detriment in our lives and intimate that a time will come when we do not use it. Now I have been reading in one of Neale's books that we should love it and enjoy what it brings and not have any qualms about it. I am confused. I feel guilty when I think I want more of it because I know I do not need it. I already have everything I need – or do I? I should so like several thousands of pounds to have these conversations published in book form.

There is nothing wrong with money, it is your ideas of it and use of it that cause problems. Your money comes in different forms of bits of metal and paper and you give different values to each piece. You store it in safe containers and safe places; you are afraid of losing it; you are afraid of running out of it. You invest it, hoping it will become more with time.

Now supposing it was perishable. Let us imagine for a moment that it is in the form of large green apples. They would not seem very important, you would store them on view in a shed; you would need to use them before they went rotten. If your neighbour ran out you would give him or her some of yours, knowing there were plenty more to come. And when you received more you would not feel guilty.

Then you 'go shopping'. You need food, you need clothes, you need something to put on your feet. Now you take a lot of your apples with you

191

and instead of having them valued or halved or quartered, you put them in a designated place for others to help themselves. Then you visit all the designated places where there are foods you need. But you take only what you and your family NEED, no more, no less.

Yes, I know, you are bursting with ifs and buts.

We have so far used only green apples as a commodity. As my people like to be occupied, they are inventive, imaginative, mainly hard-working; they have hobbies, so they do not sit around doing nothing. Each has something to give and each sees what is needed for another to do *his* job. Because a bag of apples has a value, because someone needs them, so does a warm coat have a value. Both have come from thought and work; both have given pleasure to the producer; both will give pleasure to the receiver.

But what about big items like houses, water supplies, liners, hotels?

You, yourself, would have liked to design houses and clothes. There are those who would like to create beautiful cloth, building materials, machinery. When you have enjoyed a full day's gardening you feel satisfied, happy, fulfilled. There is no pay. When you prepare and cook a special meal for others you feel satisfied, happy, fulfilled.. There is no pay.

This way of living would be Utopia. But who would do the dirty jobs, like collecting rubbish or cleaning drains? And what about the people who would stay in those hotels – they might want to do nothing for a month and leave others to wait on them!

Yes, this will be a beginning of heaven on earth. With so much being done with Love, the best will surface in each one of you and you will willingly share the jobs that you now think of as lowly. As for those who stay in hotels, if they do not become bored and want to leave, don't you think they might have much knowledge to pass on or gifts to share with others who are there, like you now go to 'Health Farms' or on 'Workshops' to learn and give of your gifts to others.

I asked you once, do you think there is money in heaven? Do you think you do nothing? Each one of you deserves the same goodness, the same love, the same joy. Remember how you feel now when you do something for another and they say, 'you have made my day'. You will all make each others days.

I begin to understand, for each time I think 'yes, but' there seems to be an answer. There would be no need for lawyers, police, insurance, but neither would there be unemployment! We would really know Freedom. I have plenty to meditate on. Thank you dear God.

TIME

Sometimes I am so bodily tired and my muscles ache; sometimes my brain is tired, or is it my mind? Does it matter that we let this happen? Time really does seem to go quicker than it used to and unless we work really hard we cannot keep up with the schedules we set ourselves.

We have sometimes talked about discipline. There are those of you who try to do far too much in a set number of hours and those of you who achieve very little. For some of you all must be now, now, now. For others tomorrow will do just as well.

If you watch a small child, it is very active for its size for a period of time, then it lies back and takes a sleep. Birds, animals and plants 'take their time'. Their days or seasons are divided into sections. You listened to birds singing to you from the trees today and you thought, 'how nice to have time to sit in a tree and sing whenever you feel like it'!

What is stopping you?

There is nothing wrong in having spells of working hard, nor is there anything wrong in taking necessary breaks. Sort your work out so as to have time to take breaks, both during the day, during the month and during the year.

But how about doctors and nurses, important goods awaited from factories with a dead line to get parts to another factory where components cannot be completed without those parts? How about journeys where delays mean lost connections and general mayhem?

Where would you like me to start! First, your doctors and nurses would not be so busy if you all took more care of your bodies, giving them right food, sufficient rest and more sleep. Your factory workers would not be so rushed if more flexibility was allowed in date lines. Journeys would be less tiring, and much more enjoyable, if more time was allowed.

Who says everything must be now, now, now? Is everything you do necessary? Are your expectations too high for your capabilities?

I can't imagine there being a rush in heaven, with everyone dashing about, but then I do not imagine there being illness, trains, planes and dead lines!

Then you will not be disappointed! You forget, there is no time. All is now, all is done with love. Think of my children who live in hot countries, or in what you call the 'outback', or in the Arctic circle where in winter there are few hours of daylight. None of those tear about. Could it be that you want too much too fast? Are you missing the beauty all around you? Have you left enough green places in your towns? Are you spending enough 'time' in your homes and with your children and other members of your families? Remember about being satisfied with your own space? Are you listening to others, spending time with them, slowing *them* down? Unless through man's treatment of them, can you imagine a bird or a cow or a plum being stressed? Now you think I am being facetious, well I am really only putting things into perspective.

There is much difference between being methodical and being impatient, between being reasonable and being impracticable. Peace my children, Peace in all things at all times.

CAUSING WORLD PEACE

What has happened to human beings? Normally animals steal and kill only for their own preservation, but this excuse cannot be made for the humans who are stealing from, killing and terrifying their own kind. Why is there so much hate and violence all over the world? It appears to be getting worse by the day and Fear is being manifested and felt.

I have not taken away your free choice. You can each choose which path you will follow. That path can be chosen from the heart, the head or the spirit. Your heart directs you mainly on a simple path where you follow lovingly along with others; the head causes you to think more deeply, weighing up the pros and cons, working out what is, you think, best for you, shows you what can be gained by your choice or what might be lost. You find reasons for your actions, whatever they be, you give them credibility.

Now when you choose the path through your spirit you become a channel through which the best ways are shown to you; the ways that help not only you but your fellow humans. It is a very satisfactory path for you find you need to make very few decisions; you find ways open up and you know, intuitively, that those are the best ways, not just for you but for all your fellow beings. You also find a great Peace, also Joy, because the feeling you get is Good. Your instinct, your conscience, your very Being, knows that the best for all is being manifested.

At this present time on your earth plane, there is great conflict between heart, mind and spirit. There is a conflict between good and evil. If you absorb what I said earlier, you will see that there really is no conflict because it is so obvious that good is good, not just for you, but for everyone.

I have explained before, you cannot stop Light, you can only put a block in a little bit of its way. At this time there are many, many blocks like patches of fog over your cities. More and more people come forward, full of fear, and add to those blocks. Now when you 'hold the Light' over your earth plane, concentrating particularly on those blocks, the fog is dissipated, the light shines through and peace begins to re-appear.

How do you send that Light? You make yourself a Channel for my Light. You fill your whole self with this Light, then you beam it to all the blocks of fog; then you beam it to those who are causing the fog and those who are feeling strong and powerful in that fog.

The fog loosens and loses its apparent blocking power for it was a nothing trying to be a something. The Light was too strong for it and the Light shines through, not just to the target patch, but to all those who are in that patch and the Light is felt by all, even the perpetrators. The blocks, the Fears have melted into their nothingness.

Does this help those of you who send out the Light to understand better how important your work is? Thought and Light are so strong and when they are used only for Good they can 'move mountains'

We have been talking about removing fear, but how do we remove the people who are causing the fear? How do we prevent more war, more grief?

You may find this hard to accept, but those who cause fear, wars and persecution are themselves full of fear. They are afraid of losing their power. They like to feel the power of controlling others. It 'goes to their heads' as you say. And from their heads they are trying to control their people, their countries, the world. First they used their hearts in living like others, then they used their heads, working out how best to gain power; the more thought they put into their plans the more sense they thought they were making and using. They have not tasted the power of their spirit nor tried using their spiritual thought and power. They do not realise how much spiritual power there is around. That is why different religions should be allowed to use their spiritual teachings, for the correct part of each religion is its use of spiritual power. As I have said before, it does not matter whether you kneel, lie, sit, stand, cross yourselves, put on a robe or just plain Be, if it makes you a Channel for my Light, then it makes you powerful and receptive for sending out my Light of Peace.

When enough of you change your thinking you will be so powerful for Good that no more wars, no more famine, no more drought, no more grief will abound. You will see the 'fruits of your labours' and they will have been labours of love. There will be no fear of anything. No more fear of Want of any kind and certainly no fear of death. You never die, you just spend a lot of your time on this earth plane, where you have free choice, in fearing blocks of fog that do not in reality exist. I will say that again, you spend much time in worrying about what is not there in the first instance. All is perfect now. All of you are loved, equally. None of you is ever alone. I AM the ALL, at all times and for each one of you, my beloved children.

RISING TO CHALLENGES
28.10.02

Yesterday's hurricane across the Southern part of England killed a few people, brought down hundreds of trees, destroyed buildings, disrupted all forms of travel and cut off our electricity supply. Did it do any good?

It also made man realise how helpless he is against the forces of nature. There are circumstances over which he has no control.

Then how should man deal with those circumstances?

He uses his knowledge, his machinery and technology and his organising powers to deal with all forms of disaster.

You ask what good was done. Firstly, under these circumstances you all suffer equally whether you are rich or poor; you all experience loss, discomfort and anxiety. You all feel apprehension and many know fear.

All these experiences bring out the divine in you. Yes, the divine in the form of love and selflessness. You forget the little self, the 'poor me', and work for the good of the many. You not only put into use your knowledge of repair work and maintenance, but you use your compassion. You forget yourselves and go to the aid of others, whether it be physically or with comfort and loving thought. You 'come out of your shells', you forget your

196

own needs, you use your beautiful attributes and many of you risk your lives for the benefit of your brothers and sisters, your pets, your domestic animals.

Let us use an analogy. All was much the same as usual and the light you gave off in general was nondescript, a sort of light grey. The storm gathered and the light became a darker grey and, as the storm commenced, there were patches of red (fear). As the storm developed the light held patches of green (I must help, I must cope). A rose colour crept in as love mingled, sending out thoughts of admiration for the helpers and love for the safety of others. Prayers mingled with all the other feelings and the light held yellow. Love extended increasing the rose and when it mixed with the yellow it became gold. It grew stronger and the light grew and grew and became brilliant gold as the love spread and mixed with the prayer. The grey was now almost dissipated and a calming blue appeared.

Fanciful nonsense? Yes, if you prefer to see it that way, but if you form mind pictures of this it can convey to you what happened on the day of a hurricane – it brought out your best and you shared it with, and gave it to, others. And now today the usual grey holds rosy tints and golden glows because of the best that YOU gave.

That is the good that was done.

HELPING OTHERS

I have a blank page and an empty mind; I should like both to be filled with something really worthwhile dear God.

You have waited half an hour to hear me – to know that it is your Higher Mind speaking to you. During that time your mind has not been empty. You have thought about many things that concern you, especially people, some of whom you have never even met. You want to take away their worries, their suffering.

You cannot do that, for though you have free will, they too have free will. During your life have you not learned most in adversity? Would you have reached such heights if you had not experienced such difficulties, such problems, such hard times?

It is because you remember, that you are better able to help others. And helping others is not to take away their problems, but to be understanding, to give them some of your strength, and above all to call them into your

197

circle of Light. When you create that circle of light and draw these souls into it, a chord, a sound, vibrates within their souls which picks up a higher vibration and enables them to better bear their burdens. It also helps them to widen their vision.

On a larger scale, this is how mass prayer, mass right thought, can allay wars, divert disasters, alleviate starvation, lift drought conditions.

So many of my children are not displaying Love, either to each other or to their earth. Destruction of people, destruction of trees, destruction of animals, all these things are upsetting the balance of natural survival, let alone progress.

Health and happiness are experienced and maintained by living in love and consideration, not by monetary wealth and possessions.

More guidance is being born on to your earth plane in the form of more advanced Beings. These souls are making a great sacrifice by being willing to descend to much less evolved conditions than they have known before in order to help humankind. You need more Teachers, but you also need to be open to their wise counsel.

When you look on and look back do you truly see much progress?

Why are we so slow to learn?

Because you are so slow to learn that you are all One. You listen to the ego. That tells you you are separate, superior, often 'above' your brothers and sisters and above your animals. Do your animals do as much damage as you do?

Animals have a 'leader of the pack'!

Yes, usually. Why do you think that is? I will tell you, it is because the rest of the pack recognises *that one* as a suitable Leader who will be the best one to lead them and look after them. They have respect for that leader because it acts as a protector, a guide. In other words, you talk about being a Top Dog and this saying has its roots in fact. A Leader should be full of Love towards all people, not only their own pack or tribe, but to everything, working only for the good of all – an example. How many of your Leaders fit this description?

Be wary my children where you follow and to whom you give your allegiance. Pray for intelligence and guidance for yourself, then pray for it in all your Leaders in all countries. Right thinking causes right action and right action blesses your brothers. When you give out love it bounces back to you and that is the best love of all.

DIVINE GUIDANCE

It will never cease to amaze me how nothing happens by chance or coincidence. It is manifesting all through my life, not only in the big events, but down to what might seem trivial incidents. I like to think of it as a testimony of Your care and love for each one of us. Please tell us more about this.

First you have to be aware of this occurrence. It is happening all the time, but if you do not notice it, you cannot learn by it. Sometimes you see what you think of as a coincidence as an annoyance, a set-back. It is when you take time to consider what has happened, often in retrospect, you understand a happening was for your benefit.

I have told you frequently, guidance is always with you if only you will seek it and heed it. I want the best for you and you want the best for you.

This guidance takes various forms. Sometimes it is physical, sometimes it is mental, but always it is spiritual, whether you recognise it or not.

When you stay tuned to your Higher Mind you become very conscious of guidance. You remember to tune-in instantaneously for help. This does not mean that you do not have free will, but you have power to tune-in for the best use of your free will.

Sometimes you are working alone, but often others are involved in your guidance. And these other souls require to be conscious of being 'needed' at a certain place or by certain people. This is when you feel particularly blessed because another has come to your 'aid' or 'assistance' quite out of the blue, as you say. You can both, or all, benefit by a happening. You look back and think, "what a good thing I heeded that nudge, that prompting, at that particular moment." You do not realise you are receiving little nudges and promptings many times even in a day. Most people talk about coincidence or say something happened by chance.

When you place yourselves under Divine Light these happenings occur 'automatically'. Your lives would be so much simpler if only you would heed all this free help that is available to all my children. The right book, the right flight, the right person, turns up at the right moment. Grasp it and do not be afraid to at least study its meaning. Your free will, choice, is always there.

Do you begin to understand that if you heed these promptings all is for your benefit, even though it may not seem so at the time? This does not mean that you romp ahead willy-nilly without thought. Use your higher mind in all things and in all circumstances.

Something to mention here is, as I have told you before, your tongue is a powerful tool, but it has to be used so carefully. Your Mind is your guide and your Mind is your refuge. Always use it with care, intelligence and thought; when necessary its re-action is incredibly swift. Other times you need to meditate on your way ahead. All this you will know by your instinct. Instinct is another powerful tool.

Be open to advice from others, but never act on that without due thought. Today you, yourself, are acting on instantaneous thought in that you are typing this at great speed; my message comes into your Mind, into your mind, into your brain, into your fingers at great speed, not letting you think. But shortly you will read what you have written and think, as you often do, did I really hear this, have I really relayed this correctly?

Yes, my child, your tools have been used accurately. It is up to those who read this to act upon it as they wish.

You are not teaching others, you are letting yourself be used as a means of them learning, remembering, my teachings. All that you have been absorbing and remembering over the years is not being wasted; you are now passing it on in a method you can use. I have told you before, we do not waste our resources. Bless you my child. Amen.

LISTENING TO GOD

Dear God,

I have been asked about tuning-in to you, about talking to you, and how to do it. Now I know how I do it and have written about it earlier on, but this will be different for each individual. Will you please explain for others, especially those who are experimenting with this, probably doubtful, even slightly afraid.

All of you are often talking to me, but you do not realise it and you certainly do not listen for the answers!

I am God, your name for Good, your Greater Intelligence of which you are all part. We are always together in all circumstances.

I am with you in your mosque, your church, your chair, your garden, your car. I am IN you, never apart from you.

But I would say this: if you have an important letter to write or a legal document to read, you find it easier to concentrate if you locate somewhere quiet. Then you really think deeply about what you are doing so that you can learn or remember. Maybe you are a scientist, trying to work out technical data. Where do you think your answers come from?

That mass in your head you call your brain is a physical organ, there to receive instructions, as are your kidneys, your blood, your heart beats. Where do these instructions come from? Why your intelligence, which is part of the Great Intelligence.

When one of your sons was very young, his brother said to him, "I think one day you will invent something" and his very young brother replied, "No, I don't think I shall invent anything, but I think I shall *discover* something."

Now that was a very profound statement, a great truth. All is already 'invented', all is Now, waiting to be 'picked up'. So to get back to your first question, you think about something or you query something, then you listen.

You are not conscious of a voice, but a subtle difference impresses you with a solution. Deep inside you, you know, you recognise a Truth. Be careful, because your mortal mind might be trying to tell you only what you wish to 'hear'.

Do not "play" with this gift, do not abuse it. Only you and I know when you are fully open to Truth. Treasure it, respect it, for it is mighty.

All this sounds difficult for a beginner.

There is not really 'a beginner'. All Truth is in you and you set out on a voyage of discovery. To do that you study reliable maps, you speak with reliable sources, you read books that 'miraculously' come your way. When they are the 'right' books they sound a chord in your innermost and you find you do not wish to argue with their truths. Question them yes, in your mind. Never accept what you cannot believe. Either it is not the Truth or you are not yet ready to receive that particular thought.

When you are seeking Truth and Guidance place yourself in the protection of the Light – that glorious Christ Light that envelops you and wraps you around with my Love.

God bless you all my children.

RADIATING PEACE

30.12.02

Dear God, I can feel you all around me and in me and I can see you all around and in the lovely people I have been meeting because of the Christmas Festival. We pick up the spirit of Christmas and it is infectious, contagious, catching, and gets passed on in, often, the most unexpected ways. Oh, that this love and good will could last the whole year through. The world becomes a happier place because the good wishes are spreading.

We are feeling the Power of Thought aren't we, the Power of Love and Light? And this is how we can project the Power of Peace that you keep explaining to us. It is so simple and so satisfying. It is no use saying to you, 'please don't let there be war' because it is we, your straying children, who are the cause of war. Does it help if I say, 'please guide the powers that be to see sense'?

You are witnessing your rose rising up, it is using great strength to become upright and send out rays of golden light. It has changed from its usual pink to a strong flame and gold colour. The rays are stretching out further than you can see.

All of you who believe, use this Light; it is My Power and it is mighty, it overcomes all fear and negativity. Project it to all places of unrest and war; then project it to all the leaders who have been placed by you, the people, in positions of earthly power. Hold them strongly in this Light of Peace. I can use you as receivers and transmitters. When enough of you do this powerfully, all around your earth plane, it is, as you said above, infectious and contagious. It can spread, it is Good in action.

Do not judge, do not condemn, try not to fear. Give out Love, especially to those whom you fear, for you are all my children and I love you All Equally.

My New Year message to you all is Be Peace, Be Love, Be Strong and faithful in sending out my message many times a day, if only for a moment. A flash of lightning is very noticeable, has great strength, spreads afar. It lights up dark places. It penetrates into the very earth. What You can do is more powerful than that! Do it.

BIBLIOGRAPHY

Author	Title	Publisher
Neale Donald Walsch	Conversations With God Trilogy & Others	Hodder & Stoughton
Marlo Morgan	Mutant Message Down Under	Thorsons
Annie Kirkwood	Mary's Message to the World	Piatkus
Louise L. Hay	You Can Heal Your Life & Others	Eden Grove Editions
Thom Hartmann	The Last Hours of Ancient Sunlight	Hodder & Stoughton
" "	The Prophet's Way	Mythical Books
White Eagle	Many Titles	White Eagle Publishing Trust

"Good God" is an ongoing dialogue, extracts of which are regularly published on the Internet at http://www.vision-unlimited.co.uk/good

Betty Green welcomes further questions of general interest for future publication. You can contact her by E-mail: betty.green@talk21.com

INDEX

INDEX

INDEX